The Drama of Schooling/The Schooling of Drama

Dedication:
To Colin Moyle and Brian Caldwell
for their encouragement and friendship

The Drama of Schooling/
The Schooling of Drama

Robert J. Starratt

The Falmer Press
(A member of the Taylor & Francis Group)
London • New York • Philadelphia

UK The Falmer Press, Falmer House, Barcombe, Lewes, East Sussex, BN8 5DL

USA The Falmer Press, Taylor & Francis Inc., 1900 Frost Road, Suite 101, Bristol, PA 19007

First published 1990

British Library Cataloguing in Publication Data
Starratt, Robert J.
  The drama of schooling: the schooling of drama.
  1. Schools
  I. Title
  371

  ISBN 1-85000-704-7
  ISBN 1-85000-705-5 pbk

Library of Congress Cataloging-in-Publication Data

Starratt, Robert J.
  The drama of schooling : the schooling of drama/Robert J. Starratt.
    p.   cm.
    Includes bibliographical references (p.
    ISBN 1-85000-704-7 :
  — ISBN 1-85000-705-5 (pbk.)
    1. Education — Aims and objectives.   2. School management and organization.   I. Title.
  LB41.S78235   1990
  370.11—dc20

Jacket design by Caroline Archer

Typeset in 12/14 Bembo
by Chapterhouse, The Cloisters, Formby, L37 3PX

Printed and bound in Great Britain by Taylor and Francis (Printers) Ltd, Basingstoke

Contents

Acknowledgments

There are many people who have played a part in the making of this book whose names will not be mentioned here, lest the list go on interminably. Of those who have played a more direct and immediate role I should mention John Tol and the Victorian Association of Principals of Secondary Schools who were courageous enough to invite me to Australia to address them on the topic of Leadership and Dramatic Consciousness. The multiple drafts of those presentations never stopped moving until I finally sat down and wrote this book. I must also thank other Australian educators such as Hedley Baere, Charles Burford, Brian Caldwell, Colin Moyle and Peter Wood who finally convinced me that I had something to say. I wish also to thank my colleagues at Fordham, especially Bruce Cooper and Tom Mulkeen for supporting me during the year in which this was written. A bow to my brother Bruce who has taught me most about theater and its relationship to living, and who was always there in the wings voicing encouragement. Finally, deep gratitude to my wife, Ruth, who endured my huffing and puffing during the writing of this book.

Chapter 1

A Fresh Look at Schooling

Something funny is going on. Paradigm shifts used to take a century or more to evolve and crowd their competitors off the stage. Now it appears that in various spheres of human activity, such as natural science, political science, management science and organizational theory, major shifts are occurring at such a rapid rate that the ascendancy of a paradigm in one area such as education is out of phase with the ascendancy of new paradigms in other areas such as political science and organization theory. So, for example, within the last few years we read about the inadequacy of traditional management theory to explain or to guide organizational actions at the same time that we find categories from this traditional management theory embedded in the policies for school reform.

Schools are being guided by policies urging efficiency and effectiveness, accountability, close measurement of tightly defined competencies, cost effectiveness, clear articulation of goals, achievement standards, the quantifying of results, etc. At the same time, scholars in the management sciences are debunking the absolute claims and the practical usefulness of this very management science. We hear much more about bounded rationality,[1] wilfulness and non-natural order in organizations,[2] organizational chaos,[3] loosely-coupled systems,[4] management as snake handling,[5] managing turbulence.[6]

These changes in management theory reflect shifts throughout the social sciences away from an exclusive epistemology dominated by logical positivism and empiricism.[7] Many social scientists now acknowledge what natural scientists had recognized a generation earlier, namely that observation is theory laden, that scientific language is inherently metaphorical, that scientific discovery requires imagination as well as rigorous logic.[8] However, the rigidly positivistic and empiricist research procedures and the language they employ remain firmly institutionalized in funding structures, legislative and administrative guidelines, professional reward systems and in professional graduate school curricula, even though the epistemologies that support them are no longer considered adequate.[9]

The language and perspectives by which schools are studied and governed belong much more to behavioristic, positivistic, empiricist epistemologies. Those perspectives are out of joint with emerging perspectives in the social sciences and policy sciences. Those perspectives, therefore, suffer from the restrictions, distortions and ideological biases of such epistemologies. Those perspectives need to be replaced, or at least balanced by perspectives that honor the anthropology which informs the emerging paradigms. This book is an effort to develop one such perspective, a perspective which employs the analogy of drama. Before proceeding to the argument, however, some additional commentary on the shortcomings of current language and perspectives on schooling may be in order, especially when spoken from within the schooling enterprise itself.

Shortcomings of Current Perspectives on Schooling

The conceptual frameworks and images of organization and management theory were most often developed through studies of either business corporations or of government bureaucracies.[10] The literature clearly delineates the differences between government bureaucracies and the more entrepreneurial industries, the former being more concerned with providing services and executing government policies, the latter being more concerned with productivity, profit, market share. Both types of organizations share tendencies toward bureaucratic formalities such as hierarchical lines of authority and privilege, specialization and subdivision of work, measurement of output, etc. Voluntary organizations such as churches and charitable agencies, while differing in many ways from business and government organizations, frequently manifest similar bureaucratic tendencies.[11] School systems, especially the larger ones, reflect many organizational features found in other government organizations, and therefore can be studied and understood and governed by means of the more traditional categories and images found in organizational and management literature.

The categories and images of the literature of organizational and management theory are of but limited use, however, when applied to individual schools. There are three realities about individual schools that are not easily captured by standard managerial or organizational categories. First their size, for the most part, is too small to suit the powerful abstractions employed in managerial or organizational talk. Such talk is similarly inappropriate, for example, for a family unit. One does not talk of the chief executive officer of a family; neither does one worry about problems of span of control, or indeed of productivity. Such terminology sounds pretentious in a familial setting. Schools are much closer to families than to large corporations, not only in size, but in affect and in focus.

The language of management or organizations fails to accommodate a second reality of schools. Schools deal with children and youth in an environment that is intentionally developmental. Hence children and youth are not expected to fit into neatly packaged identities or roles. Neither are they expected to have the single-minded attention to one task or to a cluster of tasks which other organizations assume. Their world outside of school, of course, has many dimensions (friends, hobbies, family activities, neighborhood networks, recreational activities, etc). Even in school where their involvements are more circumscribed, youngsters' lives are multidimensional: their studies vary and hence require of them many different responses; they are usually involved in one or two extracurricular activities; they are constantly circulating among either close or casual friends; they are constantly negotiating relationships with adults as authority figures, as teachers, coaches and simply as human beings. They engage in all these activities in an expected, trial and error, developmental fashion.[12]

Schools differ from large organizations in yet a third dimension. The business of schools is education, learning, intellectual mastery of bodies of knowledge. The process of education is an entirely different process than a manufacturing process in the auto industry, or the judgmental process used by a government zoning commission. The essential tasks and the way the work gets done do not conform to categories derived from business or government. Learning to use a language, learning to argue logically, learning relationships between concepts and systems, learning to evaluate points of view, is a slow and painstaking process that requires endless exercises and activities. Gilbert Highet quotes approvingly a Jesuit educator who counseled that 'the mind of a schoolboy is like a narrow-necked bottle.

It takes in plenty of learning in little drops, but any large quantity you try to pour in spills over and is wasted'.[13]

Cognitive psychologists have mapped developmental stages of youngsters' ability to use abstract concepts and to think logically. They tell us that movement from one stage to the other is slow and incomplete. Those who are able to reason abstractly, do not always do so; regression to earlier forms of concrete thinking is commonplace.[14] Although schooling for handicapped youngsters illustrates the point emphatically, all children learn at their own pace and according to their own readiness. State legislatures to the contrary notwithstanding, schools cannot coerce, or command learning to take place. The 'productivity' of a school depends on the autonomous learner more than it does on the talent and skill of the staff. Students cannot be fired for not learning; neither can they be sent to prison for failing an exam.

School Reforms Employ the Wrong Categories

The language of efficiency and effectiveness cannot be thought to encompass the essence of schooling. That language has its uses. When dealing with state or large urban school systems, those categories may be useful when considering economies of scale and when setting fiscal policies. To mount a national or state wide school reform effort exclusively around those terms, however, and intentionally to link that terminology to simplistic economic outcomes of schooling is to superimpose on schools a conceptual framework that neither fits, nor is in fact workable.[15] That language suits large systems of education in which unit costs can be tabulated and related to numbers of students graduating and pursuing advanced education. Similarly, one might use the language of efficiency and effectiveness when evaluating a constellation of state services to families. That language is not appropriate to a single family, however, because the size and nature of the family simply will not tolerate being reduced to those impersonal abstractions. In an analogous sense the size, the nature of its essential tasks, and the developmental nature of its constituency makes such language of limited use for the purposes of governing, managing or understanding a school.

The perspectives on schooling derived from organization and management theory need to be seen against a broader and deeper landscape.

Such a fresh perspective of schooling emerges when we conceive of schooling as drama. The argument of the book unfolds the human drama inherent in schooling, a drama not only of the individual person attempting to fashion an identity, but a drama of a community in the process of defining itself. The schooling process can be described as drama, not only because of the stakes involved for the players, but also because of the stakes for society. Schooling is a formal attempt to coach youngsters in the playing of the social drama, and to critique their performance while there is still an atmosphere of rehearsal (using the more traditional understanding of schooling). Once young people leave school, the playing of the social drama takes place on the stage of history where there is little chance to replay and cancel out a bad performance.

Organizational Culture and the Drama of Schooling

Within the literature on organizational theory, there has emerged the perspective of 'organizational culture'. Using concepts such as symbolism, ritual, heroes, emblems and coat of arms, these analyses have enriched the more functionalist images derived from industrial and governmental organizations. Ethnographic studies of schools and classrooms have further enriched our understanding of schools as cultures.[16] Commentaries on the organizational culture of schools, however, have tended to view the usefulness of the cultural perspective in predominantly functional terms. That is, organizational culture is spoken of as a means to an end, as a constellation of organizational elements which, when properly orchestrated, will lead to increased 'productivity' or to reform of schools. This utilitarian attitude misses the point of cultures as expressions of human meaning and purpose which transcend considerations of productivity.[17] On the other hand, the perspective of drama sheds a fresh light on organizational cultures in schools, indicating how cultural elements make up the dramatic costuming, staging, lighting and other dramatic effects used in playing out the social drama.

Teaching as Performance

Recently Pajak has called attention to the use of language and metaphor from the theater as offering fresh perspectives on teaching, supervising and administration.[18] While the sources he cites[19] and the perspectives he develops are enlightening, they seem to focus on the teacher as putting on a performance for the students, as though the students were the audience. If students are thought of as audience rather than as actors in their own right, however, then teaching seems reduced to entertainment — perhaps highly artistic entertainment, but not involvement with the students as co-actors in a drama whose outcomes are critical to the teacher as well as to the students. Though the analogy over-simplifies the differences, one might contrast the two perspectives by naming one 'Teaching as Vaudeville' and the other as 'Teaching as Rehearsing the Drama'.

Something Old, Something New

While some claim to originality may be advanced for this book, it clearly owes substantial debts to other thinkers. Those familiar with Plato's *Republic* will find a similar concern to link the quality of a nation's schools to the quality of its communal future as a society. Those partial to Rousseau's *Emile* may discern his influence on our concern that teachers stage the learning, and engage the youngsters in criticism of their own performance, as well as the performance of adults in the public social drama. So much of the book is an elaboration of what I perceive John Dewey to have said in *Democracy and Education* and other works: learning is doing; learning is living; the school is society in the process of becoming adult; learning involves the transformation of experience; learning involves experimentation, etc. Paulo Freire's work has perhaps said it better; his treatment of 'conscientization' (a poor transliteration from the Portuguese) captures the essence of being aware that the social drama is a human construct intended to serve human purposes.[20] His notion of 'praxis' conveys the sense of what is meant by intentional improvisation. Freire's insistence that education for human freedom requires that we go beyond the script others have written for us to writing our own script, both as individuals and as a people, is found in this book. Interestingly enough,

Thomas Jefferson once suggested that the American people ought to rewrite their constitution every twenty years.

Besides these educational thinkers, the book owes much to several social theorists. Erving Goffmans's work, especially *The Presentation of Self in Everyday Life*,[21] sparked my thinking about social life as drama. Berger and Luckmann's *The Social Construction of Reality*[22] provides the solid evidence for extending Goffman's thesis beyond the individual's performance, and grounds the general point of view presented in the book. Ernest Becker's work has been perhaps the greatest influence on my thinking over the past ten years. His *Birth and Death of Meaning* enabled me to understand the socialization process and the drama inherent therein, the stakes being the freedom of the individual to be her/himself within the strictures of social conventions.[23] Becker's *The Structure of Evil* outlined the drama of the struggle of societies to define themselves since the final dissolution of the Medieval world view in the bold advances of the Enlightenment, and of the role of schools in that struggle.[24] Robert Bellah in *Habits of the Heart*, written with several associates, helped to sharpen my perception of the drama currently being played out in American life between the demands of public involvement and the retreat into a privatized individualism.[25] That drama continues to unfold in the drama of schooling, as Nancy Lesko has so well documented in her analysis of one school's conflicting cultural messages.[26] Finally, the work of Paul Ricoeur has continued to crisscross my disorganized reading program over the years. His insistence that language (what I might call the script) presupposes a 'being demanding to be said' provides a depth to my analysis of the importance of improvisation. His taking seriously poetic and metaphoric language enables me to reiterate more confidently the importance of the imagination in one's attempt to improvise and to express what seems demanding to be said.[27]

There is a body of literature about educational drama that has refined some of my thinking about schooling as drama. Among the leaders in the field of educational drama one must name Dorothy Heathcote, although not all would agree with the methods used by this forceful educator.[28] Richard Courtney of the Ontario Institute for Studies in Education provides one of the clearest expositions of the learnings which involvement in drama stimulates and shows the relationship of these learnings to essential human learnings that stretch across many realms of human endeavor.[29] Keith Johnstone, a master teacher, provides a thorough and often humorous discussion of improvisation, illustrating the everyday one-up-manship we commonly engage in.[30] Day and Norman provide a good overview of the thinking of contemporary drama educators.[31] Although interesting in its own right, this literature deals with the production of school plays, or with the employing of drama in the classroom as a teaching tool, or with describing the type of learning that takes place in acting out a drama. This literature lacks, however, a view of schooling as an enactment of social drama. For some unfathomable reason, drama educators appear to isolate drama as an academic subject from real life, as though real life were an ontological, given reality, not something constructed by humans, in much the same way as dramatic artists construct a drama.

There are, of course, other influences, but the above people seem to have been crucial in seeding my mind for thinking about schooling as drama. While the book offers many fresh ways to conduct one's work as an educator, it does not say everything there is to say about schooling. It may, however, bring some balance into our way of thinking about schools, a balance which has been tipped too far in the direction of functionalist perspectives.

The Argument

Schools have a vital part to play in any society's conduct of the social drama. The social drama contains an inherent dialectic between the individual and the social environment. The individual has to understand the social environment in order to respond appropriately. Yet the individual has to be more than a mindless robot responding to electrical impulses from the environment; the human individual has to express his or her individuality. That expression, however, is controlled by the various scripts by which social situations are managed.

Moreover, the individual has to contend with the routines which social institutions impose on action. The social drama is always carried out within a matrix of conventions, policies, rules, guidelines, habitual ways of doing things. Usually, routinization is thought of as the antithesis of drama. When I drive into a gas station to resupply my car with petrol, I observe the conventions of language and the script called for on these occasions. It is a routine activity demanding a minimum of thought and 'presence'. It is not a dramatic moment in my day. However, if I pulled into the gas station with the intention of committing a robbery, it would indeed be a dramatic moment for me and for the attendant. Similarly, were the attendant my fiancée, the occasion would be filled with other dramatic meanings. Yet, even under normal circumstances, there are social conventions to be observed: one does not sneer at the attendant; one ought to say 'please' and 'thank you', and in America, something like 'Have a nice day' or 'Take it easy, now', or some such standard phrase which concludes the transaction pleasantly. These conventions are minimal ways of keeping a simple transaction human.

Schools of necessity deal with this dialectic. They introduce children into the formal bodies of knowledge by which the world takes on meaning. These bodies of knowledge in turn impose their meaning on the individual. When they are internalized as defining reality, these bodies of knowledge become the material out of which one creates oneself, and locates what one means in a world so defined. Along with the family, schools also introduce youngsters into the conventions of carrying off ordinary social exchanges. These bodies of knowledge and these conventions constitute the elemental script by which one engages in social life.

The response to the social environment cannot be so thoroughly scripted; such an Orwellian Animal Farm is humanly intolerable, and is eventually destructive to the very social environment that imposes routines on social life. The school, then, must not only teach how the world is defined, but also that the definitions are human constructs which enable humans to get on with a humanly satisfying life. When those constructs do not serve the human community, they can be modified accordingly. In other words, the school has to teach the young that the social drama is itself a human construct, the preservation and the renewal of which demands their authentic participation. If the social drama is not a drama — that is, if it becomes a mindless series of uniform routines — then it is not human. To be drama, it has to engage humans at some minimum level in a human exchange. To be a human exchange, there has to be some minimal presence of human persons to one another, by which the dignity and sacredness of each person is acknowledged, however indirectly and subtly. To participate in the social drama each person 'has to be me', and has to respond to the 'me' of the other person. Hence humanly significant social situations cannot be totally scripted; there has to be room for improvisation.

Similarly, in the acquisition and application of knowledge there has to be an individual person who takes responsibility for the act of knowing. Knowledge is not naturally given; it is something appropriated by human beings. Knowledge is not something that belongs exclusively to individuals, however; knowledge becomes part of the emerging script of the social drama by which a community understands itself and its world. Schools of necessity teach this in either healthy or distorted ways, and thereby contribute to or detract from the development of a social drama that serves human purposes. There is, then, a drama in schooling by which the dialectic and the tension between individual fulfillment and social renewal is worked out; the drama of schooling is the schooling of the social drama.

Purists may ask what type of book this is. Is it a philosophy of education, a social theory, a summary of research conducted by sociologists? The book is theoretical in the sense that it offers a coherent and plausible way to make sense out of many elements that go into the reality of schooling. It is an effort at 'social theory' in the sense given by Anthony Giddens, as attempting conceptions of the nature of human social activity and of the human agent which can be placed in the service of empirical work.[32] It is philosophical in that it attempts to connect schooling with understandings of basic human realities. It contains some evidence from some social science research, but that evidence is marshalled in the service of an interpretation, an argument for understanding and conducting schools. Finally, the books's ultimate purpose is normative, namely that educators and educational policy makers will be influenced by the values and perspectives advocated in the book as they go about the business of renewing schools.

Notes

1 March, J. (1984) 'How we talk and how we act: Administrative theory and administrative life', in Sergiovanni, T. and Corbally, J. (Eds) *Leadership and Organizational Culture*, Chicago, University of Illinois Press, pp. 18–35.
2 Greenfield, T. (1984) 'Leaders and schools: Willfulness and nonnatural order in organizations', in Sergiovanni, T. and Corbally, J. (Eds) *Leadership and Organizational Culture*, Chicago, University of Illinois Press, pp. 142–169.
3 See Gleick, J.(1987) *Chaos: Making a New Science*, New York, Viking Penguin; Peters, T. (1987) *Thriving on Chaos: Handbook for a Managerial Revolution*, New

York, Knopf; Vaill, P. (1989) *Managing As a Performing Art: New Ideas for a World of Chaotic Change*, San Francisco, Jossey Bass.

4 Weick, K. (1976) 'Educational organizations as loosely-coupled systems', *Administrative Science Quarterly*, 21 pp. 1–19.

5 Vaill, P. (1989) *op. cit.*, pp. 191–210.

6 Morgan, G. (1989) *Riding the Waves of Change: Developing Managerial Competencies for a Turbulent World*. San Francisco, Jossey Bass.

7 See Giddens, A. (1976) *New Rules for Sociological Method*, New York, Basic Books; Jennings, B. (1983) 'Interpretive social science and policy analysis', in Callahan, D. and Jennings, B. (Eds) *Ethics, The Social Sciences, and Policy Analysis*, New York, Plenum Press, pp. 3–35.

8 See Hesse, M. (1980) *Revolution and Reconstruction in the Philosophy of Science*, Bloomington, Indiana, Indiana University Press.

9 Jennings, B. *op.cit.*, p. 7.

10 See Morgan, G. (1986) *Images of Organization*, Beverly Hills, CA, Sage Publications, for a useful review of the literature on organizations.

11 See the descriptions of bureaucratic life in the American Catholic Church recently depicted by sociologist Thomas Reese (1989) *Archbishop: Inside the Power Structure of the American Catholic Church*, San Francisco, Harper and Row.

12 This aspect of schooling is well documented in such studies of schools as Philip Cusick's (1973) *Inside High School: The Student's World*, New York, Holt, Rinehart and Winston; Nancy Lesko's (1988) *Symbolizing Society*, Lewes, Falmer Press; Peter McLaren's (1989) *Life in Schools*, New York, Longman.

13 Highet, G. (1950) *The Art of Teaching*, New York, Vintage Books, p. 196.

14 See Piaget, J. (1948) *Judgement and Reasoning in the Child*, New York, Harcourt Brace; Furth, H. and Wachs, H.(1974) *Thinking Goes to School: Piaget's Theory in Practice*, New York, Oxford University Press; Kohlberg, L. (1963) 'Moral development and identification', in Henry, N. and Richey, H. (Eds) *Child Psycology*, Sixty-Second Yearbook of the National Society for the Study of Education, Part I, Chicago, University of Chicago Press, pp. 322–323.

15 See Linda McNeil (1986) *Contradictions of Control: School Structure and School Knowledge*, London, Routledge and Kegan Paul.

16 See Lesko, N. (1988) *Symbolizing Society* and Lightfoot, S. (1983) *The Good High School*, New York, Basic Books.

17 See Vaill's warning about the mistaken impression created by the literature on organizational culture that culture is a tool to be used to serve organizational ends: Vaill, P. (1989) *op.cit.*, p. 148.

18 Pajak, E. (1986) 'The backstage world of classroom supervision', paper presented at the annual meeting of the American Research Association, San Francisco, 1986.

19 Rubin, L. (1984) *Artistry in Teaching*, Westminster, MD, Random House; Sessinger L. and Gillis, D. (1976) *Teaching as a Performing Art*, Dallas, Crescendo Publications; Horning, A.(1979) 'Teaching as performance', *The Journal of General Education*, 31, 3, pp. 185–194.

20 Freire, P. (1970) *Pedagogy of the Oppressed*, New York, Seabury Press; (1973) *Education for Critical Consciousness*, New York, Seabury Press. One of the best commentaries on Freire's writings can be found in a concise work by Collins, D.(1977) *Paulo Freire: His Life, Works and Thought*, New York, Paulist Press.

21 Goffman, E. (1959) *The Presentation of Self in Everyday Life*, Garden City, NY, Doubleday Anchor Books.

22 Berger, P. and Luckmann, T. (1967) *The Social Construction of Reality*, Garden City, NY, Doubleday Anchor Books.

23 Becker, E.(1971) *The Birth and Death of Meaning*, 2nd ed., New York, The Free Press.

24 Becker, E. (1968) *The Structure of Evil*, New York, The Free Press.

25 Bellah, R., Madsen, R., Sullivan, W., Swidler, A. and Tipton, S. (1985) *Habits of the Heart: Individualism and Commitment in American Life*, New York, Harper and Row.

26 Lesko, N. (1988) *op.cit.*

27 Ricoeur, P. (1981) *Hermeneutics and the Human Sciences: Essays on Language, Action and Interpretation*, Thompson, J. (Trans. and Ed.) Cambridge, Cambridge University Press.

28 Wagner, B. (1979) *Dorothy Heathcote: Drama as a Learning Medium*, London, Hutchinson.

29 Courtney, R. (1985) 'The dramatic metaphor and learning' in Kase-Polisini, J. (Ed.) *Creative Drama in a Developmental Context*, Lanham, Md: University Press of America, pp. 39–64.

30 See Johnstone, K. (1979) *Impro: Improvisation and the Theatre*, London, Faber and Faber.

31 Day, C. and Norman, J. (1983) *Issues in Educational Drama*, Lewes, Falmer Press.

32 Giddens, A. (1984) *The Constitution of Society*, Berkeley, CA, University of California Press, p. xvii.

Chapter 2

The Central Theme: Drama

In this chapter we will take up the central theme of this book, namely drama. The work of Erving Goffman will introduce the theme of drama, especially his book, *The Presentation of Self in Everyday Life.*[1] Berger and Luckmann's *The Social Construction of Reality* fills out and grounds Goffman's work in a thorough-going treatise in the sociology of knowledge, illuminating how knowledge is both a human construct and a generator of human action.[2] Ernest Becker's work in *The Birth and Death of Meaning* and *The Structure of Evil* will be used to expand on Goffman's perspectives by his analysis of the socialization process from infancy onwards.[3] With the groundwork laid for our understanding of how individuals, groups and whole societies carry on the social drama, we will turn briefly to the terms and metaphors from the world of drama as the basic tools for analyzing the drama of schooling.

The Presentation of Self

Erving Goffman in his groundbreaking book, *The Presentation of Self in Everyday Life*, gathered evidence from a multitude of sociological and cultural sources to document how human beings engage in a dramaturgy, a staging of themselves in the presence of others. His work explained the behavior of human beings in a social setting from the perspective of drama.

Human beings entering into the presence of other persons need information about the setting, the people and their expected outcomes in order to know how to act. If the person greeting arrivals into a room is a clergyman, then one type of initial response is called for; if that person is a butler, then another response is appropriate. The situation needs to be defined. At a wake, certain conventions are called for; at a fund raising event for college alumni other conventions are allowed. Sometimes, we are the ones expected to define the occasion, sometimes we wait for others to define it.

More often than not, we need to create a favorable impression on the others present. We dress accordingly, neither above or below what the occasion requires. Our vocabulary fits the educational level of those present. Our choice of opening topic is designed to steer the conversation in directions we want it to take. The physical distance we observe between others and the deference we show indicates the respect we accord to those present. Sometimes our performance is based on a need to control the responses people will make towards us. Do we want them to see us as casual and witty, a person brimming with self confidence, or as serious and high minded? We will attempt to create that impression.

Those observing our performance will usually be inclined to accept the impression we wish to convey. There is normally a trust that we are what we say we are. On the other hand, people will be quick to notice any inadvertent actions on our part which contradict our intended performance. The shaking hand or twitching shoulder may belie our effort to appear casual and self possessed.

A favorite type of humor revolves around our awkward and sometimes bombastic efforts to present ourselves favourably. We can laugh at the struggle of a Liza Doolittle to master the niceties of aristocratic bearing and pronunciation ('the rain in Spain stays mainly on the plain'). The television character, George Jefferson, never fails to entertain in his efforts at social climbing. Archie Bunker, on the other hand, is often shown up by his children when he tries to play the all-knowing father role.

Most people would be able to improvise the typical responses of the following characters: undertaker, car salesman, prize fighter, judge, bouncer, rock star, army officer, clergyman, taxi driver, bartender. In other words, we have observed performances by people playing these roles and instinctively know the type of costume, tone of voice, diction and vocabulary used to convey that type of character.

Most men would know how to differentiate their words, attitudes, actions and posture when dealing with their children or their employer, with a customer or a golf partner, with a highway patrol officer or an intimate friend. Secretaries portray themselves differently before the chief executive officer, than among their fellow bowlers in the Wednesday night bowling league.

What this means is that we are socialized into dramaturgical conventions by which social life is conducted. Certain conventions apply to one set of circumstances that do not apply to others. There is a script for most conventional occasions. Furthermore, we learn to portray ourselves according to an increasingly coherent character. Our 'persona' (which literally means 'mask') takes shape by our consistently presenting ourselves according to our idea of ourselves. We not only learn the bit parts called for on certain occasions such as funerals and visits to relatives, but we learn how to present the 'real' person that we want to be or think we are.

Social Reality as a Human Construct

The question of what constitutes reality has traditionally been a problem for philosophers to address. The domination of the field of philosophy by Positivism has tended to trivialize that question. The sociologists, Peter Berger and Thomas Luckmann, arguing from the perspective of the sociology of knowledge, have stepped into this vacuum.[4] While acknowledging that every theory of knowledge assumes a cosmology, the authors argue convincingly that knowledge is socially constructed by humans as they interact with their environment. Every social system has a history and that history reveals the system's origin as a human construct. Throughout its history, each social system reveals successive alterations, modifications and adaptations of that system by human beings.[5] Similarly, every human being has a history, a history of being shaped and molded by people and experiences, and a history of choices and responses to experiences by which the human being created himself or herself.

Berger and Luckmann posit a dialectic that penetrates every facet of human life: humans construct meaning, and meanings define the human. Humans create social systems, and social systems shape and mold humans. Humans bring institutions into being; institutions make routines of action; humans internalize the routines and thereby legitimize them; routines define reality. Through repeated social interaction humans create 'typifications', by which people and situations become categorized; these categories lead us to expect people and situations to turn out in predictable ways, and therefore our behavior is shaped to anticipate these predictions.

Hence, we engage different people differently, depending on how we have grown to typify them. We talk with parents about family concerns — the health of aunts and uncles, cousins and nephews, or about neighborhood incidents. We talk with our lawyer about a contract, not about a humorous dream we had last night. We talk to the doctor about our arthritis, not about the speed of transoceanic shipping. In other words, the drama of life — acting out projects with others — contains built-in assumptions, all of them learned, of boundaries and topics for the script. We may improvise, but not about any old thing; rather, we improvise about things that fit that particular piece of social reality that constitutes our social life at that moment. That piece has a socially prescribed script. That script shapes our behavior, our knowledge, and defines our boundaries, our roles, our limits within that scene.

Socialization and Learning the Script

Ernest Becker provides a foundational explanation of the social behavior analyzed by Goffman.[6] He summarizes the work of Freud, Adler, Reich, von Rank, Fromm and Laing as he outlines the socialization process from infancy into adulthood. The infant, fearful of losing the mother's nurturing presence, adapts to the mother's wishes, censures and directions. The only way to control the anxiety over the potential loss of this life-sustaining and all-powerful being is to take the mother inside oneself, so to speak, to imitate her behaviors, obey and even anticipate her demands, and to accept her symbolic representation of the world as good or bad, true or false, acceptable or unacceptable.

The child's absolute need for self esteem, for having a sense of value, subsequently leads the child to accede to the wishes of other people, to read their cues, to observe their definitions of reality and value. Society thus socializes children, restricting their behavior when it appears unseemly, encouraging the adoption of polite manners, reinforcing acceptable gender behavior and censoring behavior thought to express the opposite sex. Children become socialized, in effect, by displacing their own spontaneity, their own wishes, their own selves, and putting on the face others wish to see, speaking the lines others wish to hear, and dancing to the tune someone else is playing. This displacement becomes so thorough that after a while the child can say to the parents, 'No need to punish me for misbehaving, I will punish myself'.

The socialization of children introduces them into the cultural world of symbolic meaning. Having a lot of money means something. Its opposite carries cultural meaning as well. Certain occupations, certain neighborhoods, certain ways of dressing carry nuances of value. Certain behaviors are not enacted in public. Certain jokes can be told only in certain settings. One dresses differently for different occasions. Since these symbolic meanings are the coin by which one barters for self esteem, the cultural dramatizations of social intercourse are deadly serious. If we perform poorly, then we lose our identity.[7]

What goes on in the personal realm likewise goes on in the social realm. What societies accept as legitimate authority may be based on magic, tradition, religion, law, or the secret police. What is defined as just, fair, obligatory in one society may be defined differently in another. The social fictions on the personal level and on the societal level tend mutually to reinforce one another, as the merger of psychology and sociology reveals.[8] What society allows adults in the political and economic realm can be quite as restricting as what is allowed in the socialization of infants, as Socrates found out.

Hence, it does not seem so fanciful to describe social life as the enactment of a drama. While children in their early years are trained how to perform in public by their parents and immediate family, and then by adults and peers in their immediate environment, schools are also expected to play a part in training children in the correct performance of the social drama. According to some scholars, schooling provides for those essential learnings that prepare youth to function in a modern industrial, democratic society.[9]

Robert Dreeben in *On What is Learned in School* highlights how schools, by their organizational structures and everyday practices, teach qualities such as independence and achievement, as well as a sense of universalism and specificity that are fundamental to functioning in an occupation and as a citizen in contemporary American life.[10] To learn independence, for example, requires a sensitivity to variously nuanced settings. One has to function as an autonomous person in academic studies; collaboration in some circumstances is called cheating. But how independent can one be? Obviously, one cannot be independent of the textbook or of the teacher's pet theories. Being independent in academics is one thing; being independent on the basketball team is another. Learning how to be independent in various settings is essential to carrying on the social drama. It does not seem inappropriate, therefore, to label the many activities of schooling as 'the schooling of drama', that is, schooling in and for the social drama.

The Realm of Drama

When we speak about social life as a social drama, we can describe what goes on there in terminology from the world of drama in order to clarify what we mean by the analogy. In a drama we have actors speaking lines from a script. So too in social life we have persons speaking lines from a cultural script. As in the play, where the actor plays a character in the play, but is a 'real person in real life', so too in the social drama we have a person playing a role, but the actor is a 'real person'. How real the person is in the enactment of a particular piece of social drama depends on how thoroughly involved the person is in the role. In some cases the person is wholly engaged in the role and cannot disengage a 'real self' from the role. In such cases the role's script becomes the only vehicle for the actor to express what the actor believes to be the real self.

Other elements we ordinarily associate with dramatic productions include stage props, scenery, sound effects, lighting, make-up, costume, stage conventions, etc. The play involves a plot that has a beginning, a middle and an end; that is, the parts of the play have meaningful connections, meanings and values, and even a miniature world view. The script differentiates characters from one another; these differentiations include those of education, age, sex, occupation, race, ethnicity and class. The characters have assigned roles to play. They cannot change rolls — unless there is a playful staging of a play within a play (as in *Midsummer Night's Dream*, or as in *The Fantasticks*), or an intentional deception takes place by which the social conventions of trust and honesty are violated (as in a case of fraud, or someone playing an imposter).

Mentioning the play-within-the-play introduces an important dramatic convention which the playwright uses to illuminate something crucial in the larger play (Hamlet's 'The play's the thing in which I'll catch the conscience of the King'). Within the larger social drama of public life, schooling can be seen as the play within the play; from another perspective, the drama of schooling can be seen to involve a serious drama going on under the surface, the drama of playing at life itself. That convention of the play within the play will receive considerable analysis throughout the book.

Dramatic productions involve various types of people such as the player or actor, the director, the producer, the critic, the drama coach. The player or actor 'plays at' the drama or 'plays in' the drama. One who plays at the drama does not give a convincing performance; somehow playing at the drama reveals the drama as artificial. The one who plays in a drama acts out the drama as though it were real; the actor enters into the play with a seriousness and intensity that tend to make the play credible, that somehow legitimizes it as an authentically human activity.

There is a somewhat subtle form of acting, both on the stage and in real life, which falls in between playing one's part with sincerity and playing as an imposter or a fraud. It involves a kind of playful exaggeration, an intentional expansion of the emotional response, gesture, posture, tone of voice. This kind of acting occurs when one wishes to take advantage of the moment, to diffuse embarrassment by humor, to milk an occasion of all its moral implications. This type of acting includes the following: mock indignation ('How dare you, sir!'), mock surprise ('I never would have suspected!'), a playful moralizing ('That's what happens to little boys who disobey their mothers.'), stock rationalizations ('The devil made me do it!'), and other such overblown responses. The player does not intend deception; rather the player uses a *recognizable convention from acting* to remind others in the scene that there is a play going on and that they should not take it too seriously. That form of acting intentionally exaggerates the convention to highlight the cultural artificiality of the exchange, and to remind the actors to keep the exchange light or serious enough to keep it human. The play cannot tolerate relentless melodrama; neither can it sustain uninterupted frivolity. When it threatens to go to extremes, the players engage in these mock conventions to remind everyone how the play is supposed to be played.

The director is the person who understands the drama as a whole, who has a sense of the play's unity and integrity, who has an idea of the play as making a statement. The director instructs the actors to play scenes so as to contribute to that integrity and unity, that statement. The player may have a similar grasp of the whole play, but his or her effort is concentrated on portraying one character attempting to make sense of the drama as it unfolds.

The producer is the one responsible for organizing the whole company to put on this particular play. The producer arranges the financing, the location, the selection of the director, and many other major elements that go into the production of a play.

The critic is the one who is trained to appreciate and judge levels of performance. Critics can perceive a convincing performance. They can differentiate between an average peformance and a masterful performance. They know all the dramatic conventions and can appreciate their subtle demonstration. They likewise assess the script taken in its entirety, indicating whether the conception of the play itself and its overall design carries conviction and expresses an authentic unity. Critics tend to be the voice of the community, calling attention to flawed productions, acclaiming the great portrayal of a profoundly human story, assisting the community in assessing the worth of the dramatic enterprise.

Finally, one other important person must be included: the drama coach. Most actors have to work with a drama coach in order to master all the technical aspects of acting (voice, diction, dialect, bodily expression, the variety of dramatic conventions, the practising of multiple characters to develop range and depth, etc.). Sometimes the drama coach works with the actor even while the play is in rehearsal, refining the diction, the gestures, the positioning of the body. All the above types of people will reappear in the subsequent analysis of the schooling of drama.

Three other elements associated with dramatic productions will be used in our analysis of the schooling of drama: rehearsal, extemporaneous performance and improvisation. When a play is in rehearsal, the actors and directors work at perfecting each scene. The positioning of the actors and the props, editing of the script, getting the lighting right, timing the entrances and the sound effects — all these are tried with several alternatives inserted to test for fit, for the right feel. During rehearsal, especially at the beginning, there tends not to be a predetermined right way to do a scene. The actors try their own interpretation of the script; the director likes one interpretation but not the other. An actress may consult her coach for suggestions on how to convey a certain emotion. Everyone works together to try for the most authentic or convincing playing of the scene. Sometimes the make-up or the costume is not right; several alternatives are tried until both actor and director are satisfied. Rehearsal is a time for experimentation, for grasping the intention of the playwright, for refining the interpretation of the director and the actors. It is a time for learning.

Extemporaneous performance is a form of dramatic performance. It is usually an exercise to train actors how to perform with little or no rehearsal, with no script or prearranged props. The player has to fabricate the performance on the spot, entirely from the actor's creative imagination. It can be left entirely to the actor to play himself or herself around a theme or metaphor; it can require the actor to create a character through an immediate empathy with a role (salesperson, police chief, auto mechanic). Extemporaneous performances are perhaps the most inventive of all acting performances for they demand that one make up the script and the setting on the spot, and rapidly interpret how others are or might be responding, even though there are no clues as to who they are supposed to be.

Improvisation tends to take place within a script of some kind (although some would lump extemporaneous and improvisational acting together). One may be given the general shape of a character and a situation and instructed to improvise. At another time, one may forget a whole block of script and have to perform more or less as the general circumstances of the scene appear to dictate. In another instance, another actor may forget her or his lines, thus requiring an improvised response to their improvisation. The key to improvisation seems to be the ability to carry on the scene in a meaningful way, consistent with the general traits of the character one is playing, perhaps doing some things that surprise the other players in the scene. Sometimes improvisations help to create a more complex or richer personality that the one contained in the script. In every case, the improvisation succeeds when the actor has imaginatively stretched the script with a more highly charged or more subtly nuanced playing of the role.

Both improvisation and extemporaneous acting require empathy. Empathy means feeling what another is feeling, or understanding what another is feeling. Sometimes it includes an understanding of why a person is feeling that way, although that begins to move beyond empathy to a more cognitive consideration. In order to give an extemporaneous performance of, say, a car salesman, one has to know what it feels like to be a car salesman; portraying a hesitant buyer may involve a quite different set of feelings. In improvisation, especially an extended improvisation, one has to try to read the feelings of other people in the scene. They also lack a precise script, so the improviser has to listen with an inner ear to the feeling tones behind the responses of the other actors. Do they *really* agree with what one is saying; are they feigning support for one's argument; do they want one to go on, or to go away? Those clues will enable the improviser to decide how to carry on the scene.

Artificiality Versus Authenticity

In speaking about social life as a social drama, one has to deal with two opposing interpretations. On the one hand, it makes it sound as though social life is all contrived, as though it is not real. On the other hand it makes social life sound entirely intentional, self conscious and self controlled. Concerning the first interpretation, there seems something insincere or dishonest about rehearsing for an encounter between two or three human beings. We seem to value spontaneity, 'saying what you mean and meaning what you say', being genuine, and so forth. There seems to be a sense of manipulation behind the analogy, as though we were pulling the strings that made people respond to us in certain ways.

Yet we have at the same time read millions of copies of *How to Win Friends and Influence People*. In our own minds, we constantly rehearse how we are going to ask for a raise, how we are going to dress when we apply for a bank loan, how to explain a bungled project to the boss. Even in marriages, husbands and wives read each other's mood swings to know when to avoid certain topics, how to phrase certain requests. Much of human communication involves trying to get people to see things our way, to get them to agree with us, to elicit their cooperation. Often we present a distorted or one-sided view of things in order to make our case. It does not necessarily imply lying; it simply means not telling the whole truth, or presenting all the facts.

Neither, on the other hand, is all communication so self centred. Sometimes it involves a lot of sympathetic listening. Sometimes it involves a more or less disinterested inquiry. Much of social life is contrived in the best sense. That is, it is a conscious attempt to construct something human between human beings for human beings, whether that something is a marriage, a store, a church, a bridge, a conversation, a political alignment, or a school. All social life is not a contrivance, however. Many times painful or felicitous surprises occur. On the other hand, most important things between human beings in social life happen, as a matter of fact, within and because of very sophisticated and multidimensional artifacts such as language, symbols, rituals, customs and social traditions. These are all learned, and their use is rehearsed many, many times.

The second objection to the analogy of drama points to the arbitrariness and mindlessness of much of social life. A drama implies that people are wide awake players in the action, that they are *involved*. Much of social life involves a kind of mental drifting, a kind of lethargic routine, a boring repetition of details and circumstances that are anything but dramatic. Being a player in the drama takes energy, concentration, intelligence, sensitivity. Most people cannot sustain such intense involvement for very long. That is why we have rules, routines, habitual ways of doing things so the mind can float along in neutral for a while. Professionals such as doctors, lawyers, teachers, architects and judges tend to focus with intense concentration on the drama involved in their work. Away from their work, they too need to relax that tension and reduce the intensity over coffee and small talk, a spy novel, or a mindless television show. There is ample evidence that all social life is not dramatic, that much of it is a low key moving about amidst mundane and mindless tasks or activities. On the other hand, the important activities of human life are dramatic. They do demand intelligence, concentration, energy and sensitivity in order to play the part with integrity. In these important activities (work, learning, close relationships, political action, etc.) the stakes are high. We want a successful outcome. We feel the involvement, the tension, the excitement, the challenge to be fully present to the event. That is drama.

In one sense, there is always a drama going on. Even when the actors are bored, hypocritical, mindless, apathetic or alienated to the point of cynicism, there is a deep struggle beneath the surface to be or do something of value. That longing can be buried under repeated frustrations, failures or defeats, but it is always there, way down deep. So too, in a community whose daily activities appear totally routine, there is a drama going on under the surface. The potential for creativity and human adventure may be submerged under fear, or unquestioned obedience to authority, but it will emerge after time. Convention, routine, control, predictability inevitably loosen their absolute grip and yield some ground to innovation, uniqueness, intuitions.

Schools must needs treat this dialectic. Too much emphasis on convention will smother a generation's ability to renew the social drama. Too much emphasis on individual freedom and spontaneity threatens the fabric of the drama, deprives a generation of the tools by which to understand and carry on the drama. Usually schools are weighted heavily in favor of the conventions and the categories of the social script. The real drama of schooling involves the schooling of the drama in such a way that the human fulfilment, the excitement, the zest for social life is not smothered, but rather empowers the human actors to seek the heroic, the greatness within themselves and their communities.

Notes

1 Goffman, E. (1959) *The Presentation of Self in Everyday Life*, Garden City, NY, Doubleday Anchor Books.
2 Berger, P. and Luckmann, T. (1967) *The Social Construction of Reality*, Garden City, NY, Doubleday Anchor Books.
3 Becker, E. (1971) *The Birth and Death of Meaning*, 2nd ed., New York, The Free Press; (1968) *The Structure of Evil*, New York, The Free Press.
4 Berger, P. and Luckmann, T. (1967) *op. cit.*, p. 189.
5 *Ibid.*, p. 187.
6 Becker, E. (1971) *op. cit.*
7 *Ibid.*, p. 99.
8 See Fromm, E. (1964) *The Heart of Man: Its Genius for Good and Evil*, New York, Harper and Row.
9 Sutton, F. (1965) 'Education and the making of modern nations', in Coleman J. (Ed.) *Education and Political Development*, Princeton, NJ, Princeton University Press.
10 Dreeben, R. (1968) *On What is Learned in School*, Reading, MA, Addison Wesley.

Chapter 3

The Drama of Schooling/
The Schooling of Drama

The title of this book and of this chapter is vexing. On the one hand, it appears that schooling is the locus of the drama; then again, it appears that the drama being considered is much larger than schooling. What the bothersome juxtaposition of phrases is meant to convey is fundamentally what John Dewey proposed as a view of schooling, namely, that schooling was not a preparation for life, but that the schooling one experienced was an experience of life. As one experienced that life, one was also being schooled in living, and in the process of experimental knowing that led to the continuous transformation of experience upon which an authentically democratic society depended.[1]

Living in a democracy for Dewey meant living in a constant negotiation of meanings, values, plans of actions, evaluation of social and political strategies — learning what democracy in this particular situation might look like. In other words, living in a democracy involved the very same processes children were learning in school: inquiry, collaboration, scientific verification, experimentation, group debate and consensus building, correcting past misunderstandings through new transformations of experience. The hurly burly of social and political democracy would gradually be tamed by group discussion, rational argument and scientifically verified informaiton. The taming process would always be incomplete, however, because, on the one hand, the information and intelligence available at a given time to address situations would always be incomplete, and on the other, the transformations attempted would always be limited and imperfect. In schools, youngsters would be exposed to the inherent pedagogy of this kind of democratic living by constantly building more adequate understandings of how nature, society and human beings 'work', and how they might 'work better'.

In our perspective, both individual and social life are dramatic. This means that individual lives and the life of communities, groups, societies mean something, are significant, count for something. What individuals do with their lives is important to the group, community and society in which they live. What choices groups, communities and societies make are weighted with significant consequences. That is to say, human life and social life are not simply matters to be explained by mathematical laws of physics and chemistry. Beyond those laws, there is a drama of human aspiration, longing, struggle, choice, adventure and creation. The drama involves the gamble of whether the individual and the community will achieve something heroic, something beautiful, something expressive of a transcendent quality inherent in the human spirit, or whether the individual or the community will, through some fatal flaw, pursue a course of action that is eventually destructive of the human meanings and purposes by which human life is dignified.

Drama as an art form reveals the interpenetration of the present with the past and the future.[2] As a form, the drama is never complete until it is over. While the drama is going on, the action is still unfolding toward a conclusion. The consequences of the actors' choices make all the actions that preceded them take on a particular significance. Either the actor is going to succeed or going to fail. We do not know until the final scene. That suspension of completion of each action builds in a tension to the present moment: will the course of action lead to the desired outcome, or is the actor stumbling blindly toward disaster? The actions and choices in the drama have an implied future, but we do not know that future until the end of the play. At the end of the play, the unity of the form comes together in a gestalt of insight, as we see in an instant the organic unfolding of the action towards its resolution. Drama implies a destiny in the process of being fulfilled. The action is dramatic precisely because it is filled with expectation, dread, hope, naiveté, questing — all of which point toward the future moment when the action realizes a completion.

When we leave the theater, we know that we, too, are involved in a lifetime of action which is leading toward a future. That future likewise confirms our choices as wise or foolish, prudent or deluded, significant or empty. The risk of living is that we are never sure that our choices will lead us to the end of the rainbow. We do not know whether the outcome will vindicate our labor, our risks, our questing, or whether the outcome will show us to have been misguided, blind or deceived. The intrinsic drama in our lives is that our present implies a destiny in the process of being fulfilled or frustrated. People who have no future have no way to ground their present or their past in meaning.

The drama of individual human life and of communal life involves choices. These choices are always limited by the knowledge humans possess at the time, as well as by their desires and imaginings. The choices involve questions of value and significance. Beneath the values and meanings involved in those choices lies an inarticulate worldview made up of assumptions about the way the world is and about the way the world should be. In other words, human action implies frames of understanding which give significance to the choices to act in one way rather than another. Even people we label as insane or criminal act for some reason. Though we accuse others of being 'unreasonable' we usually mean that they are not acting according to our understanding of what is appropriate or necessary.

While not the only source of knowledge, schools expressly deal with frames of understanding and with the tools for developing and expressing those frames of understanding. Using those frames of understanding, youngsters gradually move toward adulthood by experimenting with ways of creating themselves and governing themselves, with ways of creating social relationships and governing them. They not only learn the script of being an individual and the script for social life, they try them on for size and see whether they want to follow them. Furthermore, they learn the fundamental worldview that makes the script meaningful.

The larger social drama can be presented in school as relatively fixed, with the scripts relatively inflexible, and the worldview presented as ontologically exhaustive or ideologically perfect. Schools may also present the social drama more realistically as a world in the making, filled with uncertainties, fraught with dangers, yet open to marvellous possibilities — a place where history is made, not simply recorded by other people about other people. In such a drama there is a need for heroic players, for people to engage in the dramatic action of politics and science and art in order to create a new, a better world. This larger social drama is an arena of individual and communal fulfilment. That is to say, one can become involved in a larger drama that calls the individual to transcend narcissistic hedonism by means of a morally fulfilling engagement with the larger purposes of the community.

In one sense, the knowledge by which to engage in the social drama is already there. Developments in the human sciences, the natural sciences and the social sciences have provided both the knowledge and the tools for engaging in the social drama, for making history. Those very developments have also brought an awareness of the *limitations* of the tools and the knowledge of the human, natural and social sciences. They have also brought an awareness that the worldview one might construct with this knowledge is a human construct, a shaping of knowledge to serve human purposes, whether those purposes are emancipatory or controlling. This implies that the search for knowledge and understanding is itself a drama in which humans try to write a script by which the large social drama will be governed.

If knowledge itself is problematic, rather than given, so too are the forms by which the social drama is expressed. These are also seen to be human constructs, established to channel the dramatic action in a certain direction. Then the forms of the social drama are legitimate areas of study and evaluation in school, and legitimate areas of imagining alternatives and evaluating their consequences. With the powerful tool of computer simulation technology, such imagining of alternatives can generate quite specific scenarios.

If the social drama is in fact not fixed and predictable but evolving, dynamic, unpredictable, and if the worldview underlying the social drama is in fact a human construct serving identifiable human purposes, then schooling for responsible participation in that social drama should itself deal with the dramatic nature of knowledge, and the dramatic nature of constructing ameliorative forms for the drama. That approach to knowledge and intentional self governance applies both to the drama of individual life and the drama of social life.

Schooling is dramatic because the everyday lives of youngsters and adults in school is filled with small but significant challenges, victories, defeats, tensions and resolutions. There is drama inherent in a classroom debate; in the bloom of an insight into a law of thermodynamics; in the achievement of making the junior varsity soccer team; in being caught smoking in the boys' room; in negotiating a friendship over lunch; in passing final exams. Schooling is dramatic in a deeper sense, however, because the consequences of schooling are so critical both to the individual and to society. The schooling of the drama is dramatic in itself because the future of the drama depends upon the conduct of schooling. Even though we cannot read the future accurately, we can read the past well enough to avoid those scripts that lead to dead ends, or to the destruction of the social drama.

So that these mind-twisting general arguments might take on some semblance of practical meaning, we will explore three examples of dramatic learnings during the schooling years, learnings which simultaneously involve participation in the larger social drama. Those parts of the social drama touched upon here will include the world of friendships, the world of work and the world of citizenship. A brief summary of pre-school experiences and of the formal context of schooling will set the stage for the drama inherent in these three experiences. We will see, however, that these three elements of the larger social drama are deeply problematic and the schooling in them is indeed a highly contentious issue of social policy. The problematic nature of schooling in these areas simply reinforces the argument of this chapter, namely that the conduct of schooling holds dramatic significance for many players in the drama.

The Basics of Social Behavior

As children emerge from infancy and then move toward early adolescence, they move from behavior that is relatively narcissistic, diffuse, undifferentiated toward behavior that is relatively other-attentive, focused, sequenced and purposeful. Through observation, imitation, play, interaction with peers, example and conditioning by parents, and direct instuction, children learn the basics of social behavior. They learn that certain behaviors are taboo in public, that certain words are vulgar and to be censored in public, that what is allowed in the playground is not allowed in church or the classroom. They learn conventional phrases that signify good manners or deference or respect. They learn how to follow a map, how to ride on a bus or train, how to carry on the business of grocery shopping, or gardening, or serving tea. In all these instances, youngsters are learning how to negotiate the circumstances of ordinary life, and while doing so to give a good performance. They are learning how to win the applause or approval of the audience.

They also are learning that not all social life is totally scripted. When they are with a friend, they can talk about topics they wouldn't discuss with parents or teachers. They can be a little crazy, letting down the normal social reserve, laughing at nonsensical conversations, giving reign to fantasy. With parents, especially mothers, children can often be more spontaneous, asking questions, wondering why things are thus and so, expressing their feelings of confusion, anger, loneliness. In games, children can experiment and improvise, even though their behavior is bounded by the rules of the game. They find times and places to 'be themselves'. There are many occasions, however, when they cannot be themselves, cannot say what they feel, or act spontaneously.

These differences enable them to distinguish between levels of the social drama. There are occasions when they experience the joy of feeling free to be themselves. There are other occasions when they experience being totally bound up in others' scripts. On still other occasions, they feel partly free to make up their own script and partly constrained to follow the script others are writing for them.

The Formal School Experience

When youngsters come to school, they experience being treated as a member of a group, as a person assigned a role, a school-defined role, namely that of being a pupil or a student. Schools have rules which everyone is supposed to follow, and lessons which everyone is supposed to learn. There are times for expressive activities, like singing or drawing or folk dancing, but the main part of the day is spent learning what adults have decided is important to learn. One of the hidden learnings contained in the initial experience of schooling is that one is 'owned', so to speak, by the school, and by the community which the school serves. One does not have the choice not to go to school, nor the choice not to learn a particular lesson. The adult world appears to possess the absolute right to demand that youngsters submit to the everyday demands of school. Even parents, who used to appear all powerful, can be called into the school and admonished about their child's failures.

Without being able to name it or understand it, a young child comes up against a force into whose hands he or she is placed which has the right to demand obedience, and which has the right to punish disobedience. Although normally not a terrifying experience, this initial encounter with the state communicates an absolute quality to the script one is told to learn in school. This is serious business, absolutely necessary, a definition of reality one cannot toy with.

In school one learns not only what's real, but the way things are supposed to be. If one refuses to accept the script, then one is excluded from normal places within society, cast out to the perimeter where only crazy or evil people live. The message communicated is 'You'd better go along with the program *or else*'. While later on youngsters tend to internalize the script being learned in school as, in fact, the way things are and the way things are supposed to be, there lingers still the faint trace of threat of being socially ostracized for nonconformity. Schooling for the social drama is indeed serious business.

Schooling and Friendship

Schools provide youngsters with the experience of a large variety of people who are not of their own family, clan, or even ethnic group. They have to learn to deal with these others in limited time slots, to deal with them as members of groups, described in abstract categories (He's Italian; she's Irish; he's a musician, she's a scientist; she's really smart; she's only average.) They are people they spend some time with for certain purposes, unlike family members to whom they have almost total access. Through language conventions, they are able to communicate their thoughts and feelings, at least on a superficial level. They learn the subtle signs of acceptance or rejection in the choice of words others use with them, the tone of voice, the look in the eye.

Friendships grow through association with larger groups. One manages to get on a team, or to join a club, or be invited to associate with an organization. Sometimes these are connected with the school, sometimes not. Many of the basic skills and understandings necessary to begin a friendship have been learned and reinforced in the family. Schools take up what the family has begun, however, and refine and develop those basic learnings.

Friendship is negotiated through language. To be sure, friendship involves much more than language. Friendship grows, however, because two people can converse about things they have in common. Little children who do not have much of a command of language will express themselves to a friend with a hug and a smile, but the friendship will not develop very far until they can talk. Being able to talk to one another implies other elements in that drama of friendship. It implies speaking truthfully. It implies the ability to make promises and agreements. It implies sharing stories about the day's events with one another, and through the stories, sharing the meanings and values embedded in the stories. Although making friends is not taught in school, teachers often deal with those ingredients which solidify friendships, ingredients such as loyalty, integrity, respect, honesty, keeping promises.[3]

Friendship is crucial to the experience of the social drama. If youngsters grew up with no friends, then their relationships with others would tend to be impersonal and distant. They would tend to converse with them in conventional, learned patterns, following scripts they had learned about what to say to this kind of person in these kinds of circumstances. Making a friend introduces a person to one of the more profound experiences of improvisation within the social drama. Since everyone is unique, there are few ground rules for making friends. What is extended as an invitation may be rejected as an intrusion. One has to proceed initially somewhat cautiously, attending to all the subtle cues of tone of voice, body language, eye contact, status distance, etc., in order to sense how one is being understood. Attempting to make a friend makes one vulnerable to rejection, ridicule, humiliation, until one gets the signals that one is accepted.

Once one is accepted as a friend, then a whole new world of possibilities opens up. Having a friend enables one to carry on those conversations one had with an imaginary friend or with oneself. It enables one to try out things the friend is interested in, engaging in new games, exploring fantasies, traveling together to explore uncharted areas of the neighborhood, learning how to get along with the friend's parents and siblings. It also gives form to the feeling of one's own importance, and provides an experience that one counts for something with someone else.

Sharing life with a friend introduces a youngster to an essential experience of the social drama, one that takes the youngster beyond the drama of the family into a drama of being with and, in a sense, belonging to someone else.[4] That experience is profoundly dramatic for it involves the risks of self exposure, the anxiety of vulnerability, the burden of loyalty, the pain of a quarrel, the excitement of doing something new together, the threat of intruders into that private world — in short, the experience of improvising a relationship that grounds one's essential humanity. Friendships allow a very important experience to develop, namely, the experience of discourse and the mutuality of linguistic exchange. With a friend one can explore ideas and perceptions and questions. In the course of discussing something, where the formulation of a perception is exchanged somewhat like a tennis ball being thrown back and forth in a game of 'catch', two friends can agree upon a linguistic definition of an experience, a formulation of a question, a metaphorical construct that captures a feeling. In the course of their discourse, youngsters learn how to create and share meaning. This facility at linguistic expression and refinement of meaning is a crucial element in the improvisation of the social drama.

Without being able to name it, youngsters understand that social life has several levels of relationships: some relationships are relatively superficial, where one learns to speak the lines that will get one through the episode with a minimum of bother; some are very secure and ordinary, taken for granted, as in family life; some are very special, as with a friend, for they engage one's whole person in a deeper exchange where one feels more fully alive.

In all forms of social life, however, one must have even a minimal sense of oneself as a subject, and as engaging with other subjects. A social life in which all human exchange was between persons who treated each other as objects appears frightening or monstrous. That is the kind of society in which everyone is categorized, reduced to an abstraction or a statistic; one makes up a percentage of the population who works in factories; one is a consumer or a producer, a member of the opposition or a member of the party. It is that kind of depersonalized society that makes a police state possible. In a police state there can be no free exchange between people because one is liable to be reported to the authorities for the slightest indiscretion. That kind of depersonalization allows the most deceitful forms of advertising to be justified on the grounds that it increases profits.

The experience of friendship teaches us to experience common humanity. Through the empathy we develop in friendship, we are able to place ourselves in the shoes of another person. Through the experience of friendship we have a sense of value. Being grounded in our own human value, and in understanding the value of another person, we can engage them in social life as a subject with other subjects, according them the respect and dignity and trust so necessary to keep social life humanly and morally fulfilling. In a highly competitive world, in an increasingly narcissistic world, however, this kind of human social life is problematic.[5] Although schools often encourage participation and teamwork, they rarely spend much time (some student counselors are exceptions) helping youngsters to come to terms with the demands of friendship.

Schooling in the Script of Work

As Dreeben illustrates, schooling prepares one for the world of work.[6] The routine of school teaches the script of being consistently on time, taking responsibility for doing one's own work, measuring up to certain levels of mastery, being self reliant and self sufficient, working on-schedule, meeting deadlines, working for rewards, obeying procedural rules and guidelines, delaying gratification, controlling elimination, displacing personal whimsy and impulse, accepting being treated impersonally, understanding the universal applicability of rules to people differing widely in talent and background, displacing physical gratification with symbolic rewards, seeking higher status differentiation through symbolic emblems and costumes, understanding the scientific basis behind the technology involved in one's work, accepting status differentials as based on merit, accepting the economic system which defines the conditions of work. All of these things we learn, or learn to a significant degree in school. That is not to say that we understand why things are the way they are. It simply means that we learn to accept the script as the definition of the way things are.

Many of these elements in the script of workers are learned indirectly and taught indirectly simply through the scripted routines present in the everyday life of the school. Schools as bureaucratic organizations do not differ that significantly from most other bureaucratically run organizations. Schools socialize youngsters into behaviors considered appropriate for most bureaucratic organizations.

If schools were to insist, however, on understanding the human significance of the social drama, they would of necessity teach the ability to improvise in one's work, to invent better solutions to problems on the job, to derive pride and satisfaction from knowing how one's work contributes to the welfare of others. In other words, where schools attend to the human purposes served by the scripts being learned, and encourage improvisation within the script in order to promote human purposes, then they will empower youngsters to enact the social drama of the world of work in self-renewing and humanly fulfilling ways.

Schooling in the Scripts of Citizenship

When it comes to schooling in citizenship, schools actually teach several scripts, many of which are at cross purposes with each other. These scripts reflect the ambivalence and tension between scripts in the social drama. As a citizen, one is expected to participate in a democratic process of government; one is supposed to support democracy as a cherished form of carrying on public school life. Yet there is a competing script of individualism in American life according to which we are supposed to be self-sufficient, entrepreneurs, independent, self-reliant. De Tocqueville identified this tension in the American character as early as the 1830s. He saw family life, religion and participation in local politics as those ingredients in the American character which would sustain a commitment to free and democratic institutions.[7] He also pointed, however, to a tendency toward individualism which would pull Americans away from participation in public life toward a concentration on private gain and personal privilege.

Recently Robert Bellah and his associates have studied this tension in the American character and found that individualism has grown to the point where it overshadows participation in the life of the local community or the nation.[8] What people seem to want is a cozy, secure and private place they can call their own where they can withdraw from the confusion, conflict and stress of public life and enjoy the satisfaction of a rich interpersonal life with loved ones and the comforts of even modest luxuries and recreational pursuits which modern technology affords. The satisfaction of making a contribution to the welfare of the community, or concern for less fortunate members of the community, or the structuring of a more equitable share of prosperity and access to opportunities into legal and political institutions, no longer holds the appeal or even the moral obligation to most contemporary Americans. Voting in local or national elections tends to define the civic responsibilities of many, but even that population seems to be shrinking.[9]

Schools communicate such contradictory scripts to youngsters. On the one hand students are urged to develop school spirit, to get involved in school activities, to discover the satisfaction of being part of a team, part of the school family. Similarly, they are encouraged to cherish 'our democratic way of life'. In social studies they are taught the differences between democratic and totalitarian forms of government. In civic courses they are encouraged to participate in political life, in debates over public policy, in national and local elections. In some schools, service clubs and volunteer student organizations are encouraged to assist the elderly, the handicapped, and the victims of natural disasters.

On the other hand, students are taught the script of competition. Achievement is an individual matter; one has to compete against one's peers for grades, for class rank, for acceptance to prestige universities. What is called teamwork in extracurricular activities is called cheating in final exams. The ideology of individual merit and individual success tends to obliterate awareness of the social uses to which learning might be put. While the school promotes the bonding that comes from group activities, the real drama is the individual struggle for academic rewards. Grades and test scores are the currency that purchase access to the next levels of education, which in turn purchase access to the most lucrative jobs. The message preached in schools is that access to the good life, to the American dream is what schooling is all about. The bigger slices of that good life go to individuals who compete for the highest grades.[10]

Problems with the Schooling of Drama

Educators who wish to make schools more responsive to the challenges of schooling for the social drama confront disagreements among players in the social drama and scholars of the social drama about the kind of participation the schools ought to be preparing youngsters for. The National Commission on Excellence in Education believed that schools need to prepare youngsters for the life-long learning implied in the accelerated world of work and competitive international economics. The national drama to them was moving toward a bifurcation of the populaiton, with a decreasing minority of highly educated experts making technical, economic and political decisions, and an increasing majority of poorly educated citizens incapable not only of participating in a highly competitive work place, but even more importantly of asking the right kinds of questions to guide social policy. Beyond all other desirable educational activities, preparation of youngsters to handle the cognitive demands of on-going relearning in the rapidly computerized workplace defined the script of schooling, defined schooling for the social drama.[11] Similar sentiments were voiced by another nationally prominent group.[12]

Others have criticized the rosy picture of the economy and the work place presented by those reports. Carnoy indicates that increased use of computers and robots in the work place may accelerate the bifurcation of the workforce, leaving the much larger majority of workers stuck in low paying service jobs such as maintenance, security, and secretarial jobs.[13] Furthermore, those jobs may not require the complex skills which the advocates of school reform are calling for. Hence, even if all American youth were to cooperate with the calls for reform and prepare themselves for the high tech workplace, there is simply not room at the top for more than a small percentage of them. Moreover, the middle-range of jobs will have shrunk, many of them replaced by computer networks.

Wirth cites the impact of high technology on the work force mentioned by Carnoy.[14] He goes further by raising questions about the political insensitivity of corporate America to the social disparities already plaguing the nation, and to the increasing cost to the environment of increased production and consumption which the new technologies will generate.

Beyond those critics one can cite more profound analyses of problematic elements in the social drama and schooling of the social drama. Feminists have criticized the domination of the culture, the economy, the government, the legal system, most forms of public organizational life and even language itself by male perspectives and values. They point to the school as an agency that has unwittingly lent itself to the perpetuation of women's subjugation.[15] An increasingly articulate community of scholars on the left have criticized the political and cultural hegemony of corporate America over the drama of social life and of schooling for that drama. Earlier criticisms of the schools as simply reproducing the structures of domination one finds in society[16] have given way to more sophisticated analyses that utilize the works of European philosophers such as Horkheimer, Habermas, Foucault and Derrida.[17] Those philosophical frames of reference enable these critics to analyze power relationships, not only as they appear in economic and political forms, but as they are embedded in the very language we use. Beyond that, knowledge itself has become the coinage of power.

Hence schooling can express in the way it treats language and knowledge (as either a given or as a construct to be used for or against others) either an emancipatory or controlling mission. In other words schooling can continue the fiction that the script represents ontological reality, or it can present the script as a human construct which itself is problematic and therefore in need of reconstruction.

Redefining Schooling as a Drama

Whether one accepts the criticism of schooling from the right or from the left, it is clear that there is a new awareness that a nation's future is very much at stake in the way it conducts its schools. In a sense everyone would agree that the nation's future is being worked out now in its schools, not in a deterministic sense, but in terms of shaping the imagination of possibilities. From one perspective, the economic and human costs to be paid in the future are already present in the choices of thousands of youth to drop out of school. From another perspective, the political and human costs to be paid in the future are already present in the acceptance by teachers and parents of the political *status quo* as the best possibility for their children, and in their encouraging youngsters to master bodies of knowledge which communicate that view of reality present in the textbooks and curriculum guides being turned out under the influence of a male dominated, military–industrial complex.[18]

From an individual or from a communal point of view what happens in schools has a life-long effect on youngsters. Schooling is dramatic, not because a normal day in school is the potential subject of a Hollywood movie or an epic novel. Schooling is dramatic because the small choices youngsters make each day under the guidance of the choices teachers make cumulatively add up to life-long choices. Those choices, moreover, have social consequences. They have consequences for how communities will create or stifle more human social forms for their drama.

Those in-school choices have to do with being a somebody or a nobody, or perhaps a private somebody and a public nobody, or a public somebody and a private nobody. Youngsters can choose to remain passive, to allow their roles and their selves to be defined by the curriculum, the teacher, their peers, the school authorities, television, or the commodity culture. Or they can actively choose to engage in the drama as a somebody in their own right. They can ask why things mean only this or that or they can accept the textbook definition of what things mean. They can incorporate their personal meanings into the fabric of school knowledge, or be told that those personal meanings are to be kept to oneself.

Similarly, teachers can be active or passive players in the drama. They can teach science as outlined in the textbook, or they can teach the scientific material as it relates to current debates on environmental policies. They can teach history as outlined in the curriculum manual, or they can teach the history lesson as given in the textbook and go on to invite a restructuring of the historical sequence in the light of different choices the historical players might have made. Stories can be taught as independent pieces of literature, things out there to be used for entertainment (and memorized for getting grades), or they can be taught as versions of dramas of people like themselves.

Principals and others on the administrative staff are challenged to become engaged in the drama as well. How they manage and coordinate the drama definitely affects the drama for better or worse. They can treat it as a play almost totally scripted, or see it as always, every day, something to be made anew, where the drama of encouraging youngsters to reach out for a better expression of themselves, for a fresh understanding of their world, makes every day filled with dramatic possibilities.

In the chapters that follow, we will develop this theme. After first setting the drama in its organizational context, with its built-in tensions, we will consider how schools contribute to the formation of characters in the social drama and to the formation of a collective effort to carry on the drama. Subsequent chapters explore how teachers, administrators, parents and school board members can exercise leadership in playing and coaching and criticizing the drama of schooling.

Notes

1 See John Dewey (1961) *Democracy and Education*, New York, Macmillan; (1963) *Experience and Education*, New York, Collier Books. For an insightful commentary on the thought of John Dewey, see John J. McDermott's two volume work (1973) *The Philosophy of John Dewey*, New York, G. P. Putnam's Sons.

2 Susanne Langer cites the seldom recognized literary scholar, Charles Morgan, for the source of this observation on the incompleteness of the art form of drama, what he called the 'illusion of form'. See Morgan C. (1933) 'The nature of dramatic illusion', *The Transactions of the Royal Society of Literature*, Vol. 12; Langer, S. (1953) *Feeling and Form*, New York, Charles Scribner's Sons, pp. 306–325.

3 For an insightful and sensitive treatment of this aspect of schooling, see Parker Palmer (1983) *To Know As We Are Known*, San Francisco, Harper and Row.

4 John McMurray has underscored the necessity for personal relationships in all spheres of human life. See McMurray, J. (1961) *Persons in Relation*, London, Faber and Faber.

5 See Christopher Lash (1978) *The Culture of Narcissism*, New York, W. W. Norton; M. Scott Peck (1983) *People of the Lie*, New York, Simon and Schuster; Robert Bellah *et al.*, (1986) *Habits of the Heart*, New York, Harper and Row.

6 Dreeben, R. (1968) *On What is Learned at School*, Reading, MA, Addison Wesley.

7 de Tocqueville, A. (1969) *Democracy in America*, in Lawrence, G. (Trans) and Mayer, J. (Ed.), New York, Doubleday Anchor Books.

8 Bellah, R. *et al.* (1985) *Habits of the Heart*, New York, Harper and Row.

9 See van Gunsteren's essay which outlines some of the problematic elements of theories of citizenship, especially from a European class awareness. Van Gunsteren, H. 'Notes on a Theory of Citizenship', in Birnbaum, P., Lively, J., and Parry, G. (1978) *Democracy, Consensus and Social Contract*, Beverly Hills, CA, Sage Publications.

10 See Lesko, N. (1988) *Symbolizing Society*, Lewes, Falmer Press.

11 See Gerald Holton, (1984) '*A Nation at Risk* revisited', *Daedalus*, 113, pp. 1–27.

12 The Committee for Economic Development (1985) *Investing in our Children: Business and the Public Schools*, Washington, D.C.; Doyle, D. and Levine, M. (1985) 'Business and the public schools: Observations on the policy statement of the committee for economic development', *Phi Delta Kappan*, 67 (October), pp. 113–118.

13 Carnoy, M. (1987) 'High technology and education: An economist's view', in

Benne, K. and Tozer, S. (Eds) *Society as Educator in an Age of Transition*, Chicago, University of Chicago Press, pp. 88–111.

14 Wirth, A. (1987) 'Contemporary work and the quality of life', in Benne, K. and Tozer, S. (Eds) *Society as Educator in an Age of Transition*, Chicago, University of Chicago Press, pp. 54–87.

15 See, among others, Keohane, N., Rosaldo, M., and Gelpi, B. (Eds) (1982) *Feminist Theory: A Critique of Ideology*, Chicago, University of Chicago Press; Clarke, M. and Lange, L. (Eds) (1979) *The Sexism of Social and Political Theory: Women and Reproduction from Plato to Nietzsche*, Toronto, University of Toronto Press; Thompson, P. (1986) 'Beyond gender: Equity issues for home economics education', *Theory Into Practice*, 24, 4, pp. 276–283; Weiler, K. (1988) *Women Teaching for Change: Gender, Class and Power*, Granby, MA, Bergin and Garvey.

16 See Bowles, S. and Gintis, H. (1976) *Schooling in Capitalist America*, New York, Basic Books; Bourdieu, P. and Passeron, J. (1977) *Reproduction: In Education, Society and Culture*, London, Sage.

17 Apple, M. (1982) *Education and Power*, London, Routledge and Kegan Paul; Aronowitz, S. and Giroux, H. (1985) *Education Under Siege*, South Hadley, MA, Bergin and Garvey; Wexler, P. (1987) *Social Analysis of Education*, London, Routledge and Kegan Paul.

18 Greene, M. (1989) 'Cherishing the World: Toward a Pedagogy of Peace', a paper presented at the Annual Meeting of the American Educational Research Association, San Francisco.

Chapter 4

Schooling as Organizational Drama

We now turn to the staging of the drama of schooling. Normally drama takes place in some kind of theatrical space, with various types of stage space, lighting, set storage areas, rehearsal studios and dressing rooms. The world of theater also implies understandings about how people will behave while rehearsing and enacting the drama. The script is accepted as the framework within which everything else happens. Lighting, costuming, scenery, positioning and movement of the actors are all suggested or implied in the script. Small deviations from the script may be allowed for justifiable reasons, but the integrity of the drama will be compromised by too many adaptations. The drama then becomes a different one — perhaps better, but different from the original one.

Schooling takes place in social organizations which have ways of organizing available space and time as a theater company might. There are rehearsal schedules for teachers to plan their scenes, staging areas such as classrooms, rehearsal places for students such as libraries and media centers, auditoria, gymnasia and laboratories, and rehearsal places for teachers such as the teachers' room, departmental cluster offices, etc. More than that, the drama of schooling is deeply shaped by the perceptions of and attitudes toward the school as an organizational drama. Sometimes schooling is scripted primarily in organizational terms.

The drama of schooling as organizational drama involves the individual educator, the internal organization of the school and the interface between the school and the community. The drama contains tensions between personal, professional and bureaucratic elements in the life of the school. It is difficult to understand the drama of schooling unless one understands how these elements define the organizational context of the drama. In order to gain some perspective on the dynamic interface and tension between these elements, we will begin our analysis outside of the school building and outside of the school 'year', locating ourselves in an imaginary community setting in late summer.

The Larger Dramatic Context

Imagine Mrs. Smith, the principal, Miss Coro and Mr. Lee, teachers in Mrs. Smith's school, and Billy, Mary and Frank, students at the same school, living on the same neighborhood block. It is Saturday before the last week of summer holidays. Billy and Mary walk by Mrs. Smith's house, where Mrs. Smith, dressed in slacks and an old work shirt, her hair held together by a colorful bandana, is on her hands and knees, weeding the garden. They call out a greeting to Mrs. Smith who asks them if they are going to the beach that afternoon. Mrs. Smith and her husband often go to the beach with Billy's parents, who live down the street from them. All three agree to meet at the beach near the refreshment stand.

Further down the block they see Mr. Lee, wearing cut-off, faded denims and a colorful tank top, out mowing his lawn. Mr. Lee looks a little flabby; the purple birth-mark on his shoulder seems heightened by the perspiration dripping from his hair; it is clear that he has let his grass grow too long. The children ask Mr. Lee if he is going to the beach later, but he replies that today is the last competition for the model airplane association, so he'll be over at the park trying to get his plane to fly the triple loop maneuver.

The children stop off at Frank's house. Frank's father is the minister at their church. The three children are going to work on their scout projects together in Frank's basement.

Later that afternoon the three children meet Mrs. Smith and her husband and little daughter at the beach. Not far away they see Miss Coro and her boyfriend talking together. Mary thought Miss Coro was the prettiest of all their teachers, but Billy thought she was too strict, and besides, her boyfriend looked like a nerd.

The next morning, all three children and their parents attend church. Sitting a few rows ahead of them is Mrs. Smith and her family. Off to the left, Mr. Lee is sitting by himself. His wife was in the hospital with shingles.

After the service, Billy and Frank go off to their boy scout meeting. Mr. Lee is one of the scout masters. The boys like Mr. Lee because he helped them with their projects.

Two weeks later, all three children are in school. They notice quickly that Mr. Lee and Miss Coro are very formal with them, as though, almost, they did not know them. They also observe that Mr. Lee seems like a different person in front of Mrs. Smith who likes to drop in on classes from time to time. Miss Coro does not seem as strict any more to Billy; she seems distracted most of the time, as though her mind was on something far away.

The Self-Enclosed Drama of the School

The above imaginary scenes show how the school imposed its own script on the players. They come from a larger social drama with multiple personal concerns and community commitments (concerns about illness in the family, neighborhood safety, recreational involvements, marriage concerns, religious orientations, etc.). When they arrive at school, it is as though they leave their personal life at the door of the school building and enter into a different life, a school life. Exchanges about one's personal life are allowed, but they tend to take place on the fringe of school life. Once inside the school, a different kind of social life is assumed. For teachers and administrators that school life is controlled by two scripts, the professional script and the bureaucratic script.

The Professional Script

Once they have advanced beyond the insecurity of the first year or two, teachers begin to develop a sense of the profession of teaching. This is not necessarily a carefully formulated theory of professionalism. Rather it emerges from a series of intuitions gained through practical experience over time.[1] They have developed a better grasp both of the material they are trying to teach as well as a more complex understanding of the children they are teaching and their struggles to learn that material. The commitment to teach the subject matter (which teachers tend to find intrinsically interesting) is not watered down. But that commitment leads them to explore various strategies that will enable their students to learn the subject matter. In order to do that they have to relate to the whole student, not simply to some objectified mind that uniformly absorbs the subject matter as an assembly line of bottles might receive a uniform amount of liquid. Knowing the whole student, they know better what blocks attention and learning, what in the youngster's experience the subject matter relates to, and perhaps most importantly, what types of motivation work for this youngster.

As a teacher, the focus of her or his work is on this student, that student, this group of students, and on the work that they do together, namely the understanding and use of what they are learning. Teachers will talk with students about their experiences at the beach or in boy scouts, but rarely because they are intrinsically interested in those experiences (except as a scoutmaster or as a parent might be); rather, they want to know about them so they can relate classroom learning to those experiences.

The work of the teacher is to facilitate learning. As a professional, he or she develops diagnostic and prescriptive intuitions about what a particular learning situation calls for, responds with appropriate teaching strategies, evaluates whether the learning is taking place, and adjusts the situation to enhance the learning. The teacher's professional script comes to be made up of the following: (a) a focus on the uniqueness of the student's learning needs and possibilities; (b) autonomy to make informed judgements about what is appropriate in a given situation; (c) discretion to bend the rule or to interpret the policy in favor of the student; (d) primacy of the goal of successful learning over other personal or organizational considerations; (e) a sense of one's own authority based on one's professional competence.[2]

The Bureaucratic Script

Schools, however, are not simply office buildings made up of rooms housing individual professionals in private practice. They are organizations, frequently within larger, systematic organizations (the local school district, the state school system, etc.), and as such exhibit bureaucratic features to a greater or lesser degree found in all organizations. Smaller primary or elementary schools tend to be less bureaucratic and more familial, both because of size and the opportunity for more face-to-face interaction, and because tasks are not as specialized. Large secondary schools tend to be more bureaucratic because of the lack of widespread face-to-face interactions across faculty and between faculty and administration, and because of the many specialized subunits of the school.

All schools, however, have some kinds of bureaucratic procedures that impact upon the autonomy and discretion of the teacher. Weber's categories of bureaucracy include the following: (a) a division of labor and specific allocation of responsibility; (b) reliance on hierarchical levels of authority; (c) procedures governed by policies, rules and regulations; (d) an impersonal uniform treatment of all members.[3]

Experiences of bureaucracy abound in the work of teachers. School policy may dictate that a student be suspended, even though his teacher believes that punishment will cause more harm than good. Procedures for handling special education students may force a teacher to narrow educational options for some of her students. Teachers may be forced to use an inferior textbook because it meets the district's policy on non-controversial topics. Classroom time spent collecting and disseminating information for administrative concerns may seriously impinge on the learning tasks of any given day. In some schools students are excused from one or more classes for college guidance sessions or for interscholastic sports, much to the consternation of their teachers.

Administrators also tend to see themselves as professionals. Their span of responsibilities, however, extends far beyond relationships to individual students, or to individual teachers. They have more general responsibility for the maintenance and well being of the school itself. They tend to see that the school as a collective entity has an intrinsic value. It is a place where multiple resources are brought to bear on the educating of large numbers of children. The size of the student population, the age of the students and the task of schooling dictate that someone sees to security, order, coordination, scheduling, regulating, controlling, giving overall guidance, providing continuity, etc. If every student were treated differently, then where would fairness and justice be found, not to mention some reasonable distribution of space, time, personnel and money? Many legal and financial regulations require uniform procedures; creative fire drills are not allowed. Because several subjects must be taught during the school day, a reasonably equitable distribution of class time is called for. With so many people moving about under the same roof, some predictability is needed; otherwise people wouldn't know what to expect, where to go next, what tasks were to be performed where and when.

Administrators are supposed to be skilled at managing all these organizational concerns. They are supposed to have a large view of the whole school, its overall objectives, its competing interests, its underlying structure and procedures. Their work involves initiating and then maintaining the proper policies, procedures and programs by which the school will conduct its business. For administrators, their professional script and the bureaucratic script overlap considerably. While it is true, as Cuban contends, that teachers also have managerial tasks to attend to within their classrooms, nonetheless one might consider these to be bureaucratic tasks with a small 'b'.[4]

Weber's distinction between functional rationality and substantive rationality enables us to identify where the scripts overlap and where they separate.[5] Functional rationality tends to deal with the *means* for achieving purposes, goals, objectives — means such as organizational subspecialization, budgets, schedules, rewards and sanctions, etc. Substantive rationality tends to focus on the meaning of the work, its significance and purpose, its place in a larger scheme of things. The administrator's bureaucratic script tends to limit itself to the concerns of functional rationality. The administrator's professional script tends to include the concerns both of functional rationality as well as substantive rationality. That is, the professional administrator always keeps in mind what the school is for, what it is supposed to be about, what primary purposes are to be served, even as he or she administers the budget, schedule and syllabus.[6]

The bureaucratic script for administrators includes the following: (a) students and teachers should be treated uniformly; (b) policies and rules are applied uniformly for all specific instances; (c) because of scarce resources, the school must get the most for every dollar by concentrating on efficiency; (d) school-wide results are what counts (improving test scores, lowering overall truancy and vandalism levels, achieving overall budgetary balance); (e) in order to assess overall school results, there is a need for maintaining extensive records and information banks and reports; (f) loyalty to the school, rather than to individuals or groups is important; (g) one's sense of authority derives from the wider governing body, and is based on the organization's charter and by-laws.

When one places a teacher's professional script alongside the school's bureaucratic script, the potential conflicts are obvious. On an individual level for every teacher, there is a constant dramatic tension between one's professional script and the bureaucratic script. There is no resolution to this tension as long as teachers work within the traditional, institutional school setting. Individual attention to the student, either for instructional or disciplinary remediation, will always be limited by the institutional demands of the setting.[7] One's professional tendencies will always want to give more time to certain students, but the schedule will not allow. Compromises based on what the setting will allow define the agenda of everyday life in school. The loss of professional autonomy is the root source of teachers' alienation from the institution; it can be overcome only by creative teachers who know how to use the institution to benefit youngsters more often than the institution can defeat their autonomous professional action. Since teachers normally feel a deeper commitment to their professional script, they will chafe under the daily intrusions of the bureaucratic script.

The Internal Organizational Level

Beyond the personal level, there is a drama going on in the organization as such. That drama involves whether the school will be able to function according to its substantive purposes or whether it will allow the bureaucratic script to dominate its substantive purposes.[8] In every organization, there is a tendency for the bureaucratic script to become an end in itself, to define the total reality of the institution.

Rules, instead of providing guidance for common sense, can oppress common sense in a misguided insistence on absolute uniformity. Subunit specializations such as departments can define their own domain as though encompassing the totality of schooling. Concern for coordination expressed in a superabundance of planning meetings can so drain teachers' energies that although nothing may be left to chance, nothing may be left for spontaneity and the integrity of the discipline.

The drama of organizational life is about the struggle against rigid uniformity, about resisting the suppression of uniqueness and individuality, about rebelling against the freezing of the organizational script in one bureaucratic form. If the organization is to be humanly alive and serving human purposes, then there will always be tension between the demands of predictability and the necessity of flexibility, between the need for control and the need for responsiveness to emerging needs and opportunities, between routine and innovation. In other words, organizational life is thought to function optimally when everyone knows and follows the script: when the work is done well, on time, on budget, according to specifications, by the people expected to do the job; when reports are filed according to standard formats, on schedule, accurately; when meetings are run according to the agenda, with a minimum of conflict and acrimony; when the everyday rituals are followed harmoniously and uniformly. Such an idealized state of affairs hardly ever obtains, however.

In the case of schools, such an idealized state would violate the normalcy of young people who are seldom predictable, seldom on time, seldom accurate, seldom not in some kind of conflict, seldom 'within budget' and never uniform. Schools try to socialize them into being more predictable, being on time, being accurate. But if those tasks become the only agenda for the school, then the school fails in some of its other essential purposes, such as nurturing creativity, inquisitiveness, self reliance, respect for differences, democratic attitudes and practices, inventiveness, risk-taking. Hence the drama of organizational life is lived within the tension between bureaucratic demands and the developmental learning tasks of youngsters. The bureaucratic script can never be so rigid as to preclude improvisation.

Within the overall script of playing school, both teachers and students are constantly improvising. Every student is unique, due to genetic, hereditary, familial and prior educational experiences. He or she brings to every learning task unique variables of readiness, interests, motivations, associations, attitudes, moods. While there is a common content within the curriculum, what each student apprehends will be nuanced by his or her unique attributes at the time of the learning tasks. How a youngster puts that learning to use, relates that learning to previous learnings, brings it into some kind of organic connection with a general set of understandings and values about the world — that will not be totally controlled by the teacher or the textbook. In that sense, the script to be learned will always be personalized, even if, in an extreme case, the school were to discourage such personalized learning.

Standardized tests, as well as some teacher constructed tests can appear to reward only the uniform 'right answer'. On the other hand, the whole point of the learning task is *that it be personalized*. Testing the learning of the group must attempt to surface a common content of the learning. The expression of that commonly shared content, however, should presume a personalized appropriation of that content by each person, who, for the purpose of revealing what has been learned, expresses that learning in the agreed-upon format by which the knowledge can be shared in common.

After youngsters repackage the more superficial, common content of the group learning for classroom and standardized tests, their learning frequently becomes atrophied because they are not asked to do anything with it that would make it personally useful or significant to them. Whether the learning involves an understanding of a metaphor used in a poem, an appreciation of the political conflict embedded in an episode of history, an insight into the chemical properties of a compound, or the grasp of the logic of the model problem in a geometry class, it will tend to evanesce after the test of the common content unless the student is stimulated to see its significance for his or her life.

The organizational drama of schooling fails to come alive if the script of schooling is defined simply by the common content of the curriculum. The script of schooling is never fully written ahead of time; the curriculum and the common content is forever an incomplete script. Each student completes the script by appropriating the material to be learned and then by expressing in some personalized form what that learning means for her or his life and for the lives of those around. That is to say, learning is not like some uniform liquid that is poured into a bottle and then is calibrated by pouring out of that bottle the same amount of liquid into a measuring cup. It is rather something that enters my life, becomes a part of me, the way nutrients from a meal enter my blood stream, become part of me and, even more, become part of my life that I can share with others. In other words what I learn becomes incorporated into the script I am writing or that we are writing as we engage in various kinds of social exchange. That is why the drama of schooling is the schooling of drama; it is a community's effort to teach youngsters how to work within the general framework of a common script (the culture, community traditions, general moral norms, commonly accepted language usage, etc.), but to improvise within that script to create something uniquely human among their fellows. More will be said of this in the next chapter.

The point to be made here is that the essence of schooling as an organizationally conditioned drama lies in the organization's ability to promote a genuine drama, rather than a totally predictable, endlessly uniform, robot-like performance. To identify the common content of learning which can be tested through the uniform responses on tests as the whole of schooling is a tragic mistake. It is to confuse a half script for the whole play. Some would say that it is to confuse a bad script for the real or potential play.

Similarly, teachers improvise within the script. To be sure, they see to the learning of the common content of the curriculum. Even to achieve that modest goal, however, teachers are remarkably inventive. They constantly check to see whether the student is blocked in the learning task. What will unblock the student? Is it a question of motivation? What normally motivates the youngster? Is the problem in the stimulus itself — perhaps the textbook vocabulary is too abstract? Perhaps a puppet show will demonstrate the point of the lesson. Teachers know that learning tasks must make sense to youngsters, so they constantly present their potential material in ways that go beyond the textbook. If a teacher were to stick to the script provided by the syllabus and the textbook, then many, if not most of the students would fail to learn. 'Teacher-proof' curricula, textbooks, instructional protocols, assessment procedures — all assume erroneously that the script of schooling can be completely written ahead of time.

When it comes to the more complex task of encouraging youngsters to complete the script of the learning episode, improvisation becomes even more important. Teachers have to create situations which will tease, engage, nudge the student to express what he or she has learned in exchanges with other students. Perhaps it might involve using the metaphor from the poem in the opening section of a mystery story which the teacher asks three students to compose on the spot. Perhaps it might take the form of using the metaphor to describe a personal experience. Teachers carry around with them an assorted 'bag of tricks' which they can call upon in given circumstances to enhance the learning at hand. More often than not, the better teachers will constantly try out new games, new puzzles, new ways to bring the learning out into a dramatic exchange.[9]

Hence, the organizational drama of schooling must encourage improvisation within the general script provided by the curriculum and by school policies. When either students or teachers are unable to improvise then they perform according to prescribed roles; their performance is wooden, predictable, uniform. The life goes out of the drama; the script defeats the drama; the script defeats itself, for it destroys the very thing it was intended to serve, namely the human exchange between developing youth and the adult community in which youngsters learn with ever increasing facility how both to be themselves and to be responsible for the drama of the community's journey toward a richer experience of its own humanity. Those two motifs make up the substance of the drama of schooling. As an organization, schools should be tightly coupled around those motifs.[10] In order to function with appropriate discretion in pursuit of those generous goals, however, teachers and students need to work within a relatively loosely coupled script. They have to be able to write part of the script themselves, for it is *their* drama as much as it is the drama of the larger society.

The Drama of the School and the Community

The interface between the school and the community provides still other ingredients for the organizational drama of schooling. The school, first of all, operates under the jurisdiction of the school board, which in turn, is usually a body of people selected by the community to represent their interests in the schooling of their children. The school board operates within guidelines and laws established by the State, which is the primary legal entity responsible for establishing and maintaining schools. There are many interest groups, however, who seek to influence the school. Those interest groups include business organizations such as automobile manufacturers, banks and houseware utensil companies which seek to have the school include in its curriculum various consumer oriented learning experiences. The League of Women Voters, The Elks Club, The American Civil Liberties Union, Planned Parenthood, The Society for the Prevention of Cruelty to Animals, The United Nations, Mothers Against Drunk Drivers, The Sierra Club, The Legion of Decency — these are but a few of the groups who wish to promote a point of view through the schools. Beyond these groups there are racial, religious and ethnic communities which seek to influence how children are treated in school and what gets taught in school. Regulatory governmental agencies such as the Environmental Protection Agency, the Labor Department, the Drug Enforcement Agency and the Department of Justice also influence life in schools. In other words, the school is not a play unto itself. The larger drama in society constantly intrudes, for better or for worse.

Sometimes the intensity of the drama in society seriously disrupts the life of the school. Enforcement of school desegregation brought racial tensions and sometimes violence into the schools. The recent widespread use of cocaine and crack is another example of destruction elements in the larger community invading the life of schools. On the other hand, we can point to instances where groups in the local community asserted themselves and worked for the improvement of schools which were in various stages of disintegration. National reform efforts, whether progressive or conservative, have set in motion in state after state new legislation and new funding for school improvement.

From our perspective, however, it is at the individual school level and its interface with its local community that we believe the analogy of drama is best suited. It is at that level that parents with children in the school get involved. It is at that level that school administrators and staff members reach out into the community for face-to-face exchange with people in the community. Sometimes that exchange involves invitations to become involved in a school–community cooperative effort, such as a walkathon for Children with AIDS. Sometimes it involves appealing to local neighborhood leaders to help the school defuse a tense ethnic or racial confrontation. Sometimes it involves a request for a community resource person to speak at a school assembly.

In the give-and-take between a school and its local community, the school stays in contact with the social drama for which it is preparing its youngsters. If there are racial problems in the community, then the school can actively deal with those problems in the school, analyzing the scripts each side imposes on the other, exploring the stages on which the drama in the community is played out (in segregated housing patterns, in employment opportunities), in comparing cultural expressions such as music and family patterns. If there are environmental issues being debated in the community, then the school can use that example as a learning laboratory for scientific and political analysis. Insofar as there are conflicts between the community and the school (for example, over evolutionary theories in biology textbooks), then that will heighten the drama of that particular area of schooling, calling into question the scientific and religious scripts which people employ to make sense out of their world.

For the schooling of drama to work, the school has to be attentive to the drama taking place in the social life of its community. 'Playing school' seems unreal when school is conducted as though the outside community didn't exist. Not only should teachers draw on examples from the community, examples of courageous behavior, of democratic processes at work, etc., but they should point to those parts of the social drama in their community that usually do not work for the people involved. In other words, a school can prepare its youngsters to participate in that drama to make it a more humanly supportive environment. The schooling of drama cannot succeed if it is totally withdrawn from the larger social drama. The drama played out in the school has to be fed by the drama taking place in its community.

Recapitulation

The drama of schooling can be seen as the drama inherent in assigning individuals to this kind of setting with these kinds of intra- and inter-organizational dynamics going on and placing in their hands the preservation and development of the human social drama itself. Given everyone's need to create their own autonomous character within all the limitations of their script, and the need for the school community to recognize its responsibilities to its larger script of promoting the common good, can they reconcile the needs of both? Beyond that, can they recognize that the drama is itself a human construct, the discipline of which is to serve profoundly human purposes, and that an essential part of the schooling of youth is to learn how to preserve and improve that drama through their common improvisation within the yet-to-be-completed script?

Notes

1 For a good account of how practitioners learn on the job see Donald Schon (1983) *The Reflective Practitioner: How Professionals Think and Act*, New York, Basic Books. See also, Sergiovanni, T. (1986) 'Understanding reflective practice', *Journal of Curriculum and Supervision*, 6, 4, pp. 355–365.
2 See Corwin, R. (1965) 'Professional persons in public organizations', *Educational*

Administration Quarterly, 1, 3, p. 7. For an application of this concept to teachers, see Sergiovanni, T. and Starratt, R. (1988) *Supervision: Human Perspectives*, 4th ed., New York, McGraw-Hill, pp. 64–66.

3 See Max Weber (1947) *Theory of Social and Economic Organization*, Henderson, A. and Parsons, T. (Trans), New York, Oxford University Press, pp. 333–336.

4 For a thorough analysis of this overlapping, see Larry Cuban (1988) *The Managerial Imperative and the Practice of Leadership in Schools*, Albany, NY, State University of New York Press.

5 See Eisenstadt. S. for a helpful elaboration on this distinction in his edition of Weber's writing (1968) *Max Weber: On Charisma and Institution Building*, Chicago, University of Chicago Press, pp. li–lv.

6 Cuban, *op. cit.*, makes this point well.

7 Cuban, ibid., again underscores this basic challenge.

8 Cuban, ibid.

9 A good example of one great teacher's imaginative approach can be found in Kenneth Koch (1973) *Rose, Where Did You Get That Red?: Teaching Great Poetry to Children*, New York, Random House.

10 See Weick, K. (1976) 'Educational organizations as loosely coupled systems', *Administrative Science Quarterly*, 21, 2, pp. 1–19.

Chapter 5

The Drama of Schooling:
The Formation of a Character

Schools help to form the characters who will engage in the social drama. While they are not the only institutions engaged in the formation of character, they have traditionally assumed that as a primary purpose.

'Character' is a word educators and parents often discuss. Character, of course, would carry cultural nuances; what the word signifies in a Prussian military school would differ from the meaning given in a Buddhist monastery. In the West, its popular meaning has to do with qualities like honor, courage, perseverance, principled behavior.[1] A strong character is considered to signify one who can withstand hardship and temptation, who can persevere against difficult obstacles, who can place principle above personal convenience and pleasure. A weak character, on the other hand, is thought to be one who gives in easily to pressure or resistance, takes the easy way out, neglects responsibilities in favor of self indulgence.

Another meaning of the term character, much closer to the one we are developing in this chapter, has to do with a person who exercises a degree of individuality. People remark, 'He's a real character', when the person in question stands out from the crowd, does not conform to expected protocols, draws attention by exaggerated gestures to unusual qualities he possesses. Usually such statements convey either a certain disapproval of the 'character's' flaunting of social traditions, or a certain envy of the 'character's' spirited disregard for unnecessary formalities.

Sometimes the term character is used to signify a social role or stereotype. People sometimes say, 'He's a likeable enough character', meaning thereby that someone they meet on a superficial basis, whom they neither know nor care to know, is pleasant, inoffensive, but not particularly interesting. He is a background character in a set, one who is incidental to the drama.

Schools form characters in all the above meanings of the term. The focus in this chapter, however, is on the formation of a distinct human person who knows how to act and to find meaning within the social drama. The formation of a character, therefore, refers to the challenge schools face in attempting to equip a youngster with the necessary conventions and understandings of the social drama, while at the same time encouraging that youngster to discover who he or she wants to be. To put it another way: the school must enable the youngster to create him or herself at the same time the youngster is learning those common meanings by which to conceal, protect and express the self in social life. Paradoxically, even when schools fail to attend to this extraordinarily difficult task, students frequently succeed at it, although usually imperfectly, and at a painful cost.

The Family Socialization of Performers

Children arrive at school already trained as performers. Within the family, they have already learned how to negotiate the drama of family life. They have learned work scripts, sexual scripts, health scripts, scapegoating scripts, religious scripts, even rudimentary economic and political scripts. By observation and trial and error, they have learned status and role cues: how to please grandma, how to talk with the mailman, how to dress and fold one's hands in church, how to behave at the dinner table when guests are present.

Children have learned to perform in a social drama, because it is in the social drama that the underlying, most important element in a child's life is negotiated: self esteem. As was mentioned earlier, the most fundamental urge and instinct of human beings, around which all forms of human development takes place, is self esteem.[2] Under normal circumstances, an infant finds itself totally supported and held in the embrace of its mother. She is the source of food, warmth, security, delight. The infant experiences itself as an object of attention and affection. Without understanding it, the infant experiences a sense of ultimate value. As the child begins to become an 'I' (an actor) as well as a 'me', (a passive receiver) the child seeks to explore and express itself freely and naturally. In this attempt at exploration and expression, the child is increasingly thwarted by the mother who threatens to withdraw her approval unless the child refrains from certain behaviors and embraces other behaviors which the mother demands. The child experiences a basic anxiety of being separated from what it knows as the source of its life, the omnipotent mother. In order to reduce that anxiety, the child learns to displace its own spontaneous actions in order to please the mother. As the trial and error of everyday life progresses, the child becomes more and more adept at perceiving what brings approval and what brings disapproval. That perception becomes increasingly mediated by language and symbol. Again, without being able to comprehend what is happening, the child gradually learns to displace more and more of its own spontaneous activity in favor of maintaining the approval of the mother.

Over time, the child learns that other adults in the environment likewise will exchange their approval for the child's accession to behaviors that please or accommodate them. This is what is called socialization, namely, that the child is gradually shaped to conform to the norms, customs, traditions and rituals of its immediate adult society.

Depending on the severity with which this socialization was carried out, the child will arrive at his entry to school with little, some, or, in a few cases, much of his or her self intact. Socialization is a process of displacing the self in preference to the demands of adult society. That process forces the question every child must face: 'Whence will I derive my self-esteem? Will it come from myself, from experiencing my own competency to do and make and invent? Or will it come from without, from the approval I get from other people for doing what they want of me?' Even within the mother–child relationships there is normally a protracted, sometimes never ending struggle — on the one hand the child wanting to assert its own will; on the other, the mother attempting to force the child to do 'the right thing', 'the acceptable thing', to avoid being naughty, or disrespectful, or dirty.

The 'I' who arrives at school is a socialized 'I' to a greater or lesser degree. That means that the character is partially a social creation of his family and immediate community. The child has learned to perform. Insofar as the script for that performance has been internalized, the character is considered normal. But insofar as the normalcy is an automatic, nonreflective performance, it is unathentic. It is not the free expression of this unique person; rather, it is a form of neurosis, because it is a form of self displacement.

This is the paradox of socialization — that earliest engagement in the social drama — that it inhibits the individuality of the person, robs the person of self reliance and places the control of one's self esteem in the hands of others. Socialization is cultural. That is, it is derived from the norms, customs, traditions, symbolic values of the culture. To be enculturated, then, is to a greater or lesser degree to accept others' definition of right and wrong, good and bad, beautiful and ugly, success and failure, honor and dishonor, and to apply those definitions to oneself.

Underlying the quest for self esteem is an inarticulate yet relentless search for self value. This search is driven by a profound sense that one's life is not an accident, a meaningless occurrence tossed up in the cauldron of evolution. It is a search to be recognized as a primary object of value in the universe.[3] Children want to know not only that they belong to this or that group, family, clan or tribe; they want to know what specific and unique contribution they are expected to make. Such a quest is fundamentally a quest to write one's story heroically. While children may fantasize themselves performing extraordinarily heroic deeds, they will settle for lesser forms of heroism in their real lives. They simply need to be a *somebody*.

Being a somebody is symbolically negotiated. It takes place in a system of meaningful action and words. Being a somebody is a cultural construction; hence, it is learned in and through the culture. Yet, being a hero can be a highly narcissistic endeavor. One has constantly to compare one's recognition with what is accorded to others. One point in the batting average, one one-hundredth of a point in the grade average, one more scout badge than one's rival — all this seemingly insignificant slicing up of the symbolic reward and recognition system is deadly serious business to the establishing of self worth.

Culture provides those rules, cues, customs and distinctions that enable a person to protect self esteem and seek heroic satisfaction. Culture provides the definitions of success, of excellence, of value. Within the culture, subcultures, such as found among adolescents, further refine those rules and distinctions. Within some cultures, counter-cultural groups develop other definitions of success, excellence and value. Street gangs, motorcycle gangs, ethnic clubs, country clubs all have their ways of distinguishing themselves as heroic in counterdistinction to the popular or general culture.

The youngster who arrives at school for the first time is therefore one whose character has been partly formed. Being in school, however, requires a new level of socialization. The child has to adjust to a new set of adults outside of the warm and familiar aura of the family, and to a large number of other children who are complete strangers. There are new rules, new tasks, new definitions of success, new reward and punishment systems — in effect, a new culture to be mastered.

For the school's part, it has to decide what it wants to make of these defenseless and malleable children. Does it want absolute uniformity? Then it will create a climate in which there are only right and wrong answers, good and bad behaviors, and reward systems which immediately reinforce the right answers and the good behaviors, and punish the wrong answers and the bad behaviors. In other words, the school will present a script that allows no interpretation, no improvization, no deviation. They will form characters who will engage in a social drama that presumably is totally controlled; characters with no unique personal centers, characters whose quest for heroism is satisfied by the external rewards of being right and good more often than being wrong and bad. Whether the children will allow a school so to control them is another story. More than a few healthy characters have been formed precisely by being forced to resist such efforts of a school to control them. Where children have been socialized at home to respect and obey those in authority, however, such schools have an easier time bringing children to an unquestioning conformity.

Other schools may seek more of a middle ground in the formation of a character. Demands for conformity to rules, traditions and customs will be balanced by encouragement in self expression and self development. However, such self expression may not be conceived so much as a preparation for participation in the social drama. It may simply be thought of as an important part of the person's private sense of fulfilment. In other words, creative self expression may be thought of as a legitimate pastime for internal self enrichment, but not for one's public life. In that arena, cultural forms of acceptable behavior are to be followed quite rigidly.

Finally, we can conceive of schools who intentionally take up the challenge of forming a character who can integrate self expression and self development with the public agenda of social life. In such schools, children are taught the customs, the conventions, the accepted ways of understanding the world. But they are also encouraged to make their own way in that world, to engage public life and its demands on one's own terms.

Being an authentic person in public life is a very complicated business.

Small children will attempt it in terms that make sense to them: older children and adolescents will attempt it in different ways that make sense to them. Piaget,[4] Kohlberg,[5] Erickson,[6] and others have mapped the terrain of stages of development which children and youth go through on their journey toward adult maturity. Each stage has relatively discrete ways of responding to the world, or of framing basic questions and tasks for oneself. Schools attempting to form characters who integrate self expression with the accepted scripts of public life will be sensitive to the possibilities of and limitations on such integration which the youngsters' stages of growth allow.

Individual Self Expression

Pursuing our analysis further, we may focus for the moment on the formation of a character who speaks for him or herself. Besides teaching the accepted linguistic conventions and labels of things and traditional frameworks for viewing how the world makes sense, schools can spend the necessary time encouraging youngsters to describe their experiences and meanings in their own words and images. Written and oral reports, in which youngsters are learning the mastery of language, can include a greater concentration on the youngsters' personal world. This encouragement provides a basic legitimacy to their perceptions, and enables them to value their perceptions in their own right. Children need a forum to speak their own truth, and to have that truth valued. As they attempt to communicate what that truth means to them, they will necessarily be forced to use linguistic and visual symbols common enough to be understood.

Similarly, the ordinary problems, dilemmas and crises that occur in the lives of children (a spilt glass of milk, a fight in the school yard, being called an insulting name, having a disagreement with a parent, breaking a school rule and being reprimanded) can become the occasion of learning both the social conventions embedded in the social script as well as their own way of making that script work for them. The teacher can stop the action, focus the attention of the group on what has happened and have them discuss how they see the problem. It may also help to rehearse the scene, to have the students play the scene differently, so that the problem is solved, or the crisis averted. Such relatively simple classroom interventions help youngsters get a sense of how they feel inside, who they want to be, what they want out of a particular situation, and then, on reflection, to judge whether their actions were worth all the ensuing consequences. It enables them experientially to know that they have it in their power to act differently, that they can act in such a way as to express themselves as well as satisfy the demands of the social situation.

Improvisation as Expression of Character

Most of the time we are not aware that we are playing a role or that we are speaking lines written by the culture. We think that we are being our true selves most of the time. Very often, however, we fall into stereotypical responses to situations; we repeat lines we have seen our parents use in similar situations; we act in ways we have seen others we have admired (frequently movie and television actors) act; we say what we think is called for by the situation, or what will create a favorable impression on others. We do all this thinking we are acting spontaneously, but we are repeating phrases and gestures we have learned to use in other situations. There is an economy to acting in this way. We save ourselves the trouble of seeing the novelty in each situation, of noticing the uniqueness of each person, of speaking to the special circumstances to be discovered in everyday events. By treating situations, people, events under general categories, we provide the appropriate general response and get on with our own business.

It takes much more energy and concentration to see the people we encounter and the chance happenings that occur with fresh appreciation. Responding to those encounters and happenings with a genuine piece of ourselves requires taking the time to regard them in their uniqueness. It requires an opening of ourselves to them, letting them come inside us and touch us and *then* call forth a response from us. That response then has to be much more genuine and personal. Our response, while employing conventions of language and gesture, must express ourselves in our uniqueness, even if it involves an awkward searching for the right words to express our sentiments. Improvisation in this sense implies a creative communication that is honest and self revelatory.

Oddly enough, the stock responses prevent our true character from being touched or revealed. Our essential character is revealed much more when we have to make up new lines that best express a genuinely felt response. As we do this more often, we approach the moral sense of the word 'character', because there is now a fundamental honesty to our words and gestures. The Socratic adage, 'Know thyself', which was always related to the beginning of virtue and character, now comes to mean something. To be a true character, we must know ourselves. We must be comfortable with who we are and speak from the center of who we are. Often we know that center by contrast, when we speak lines that conflict with ourselves. We say, 'That wasn't me'. 'I didn't feel myself when I did that'.

Becoming a character, then, requires creative recognition of the uniqueness of events and people as well as our spontaneous reaction to them. People will come to know us as we are in so far as we are able to improvise with words and gesture that reveal our true selves and at the same time reveal something of *their* own truth. In a sense, we create our selves by saying who we are; sometimes we say who we are through the gentle tenderness by which we accept the fragile beauty of the other. We reveal ourselves by giving back to the other the truth that we appreciate about the other. We give form and substance to our character through the creative improvisation of the unique lines that are ours, and only ours to speak. The truth that they reveal is always truth that points in two directions; hence character is always revealed in relationship.

Self Expression in Special Talents and Interests

Most youngsters have one or more special hobbies or interests. These interests usually are the special ways youngsters have of becoming a somebody. Normally they get to know all they can about a given interest, whether it be stamp collecting playing basketball, or butterflies. By mastering something so thoroughly, they develop a sense of competency; they know that they can do something well; in this particular area, they are someone special.

Frequently these interests and hobbies can be related to what is happening in school. By celebrating the expertise exhibited in these special interests, schools nurture that sense of mastery which is so essential to becoming a person in one's own right. As one grows older, new interests replace fomer ones; the need to be appreciated for the special talents which those interests exercise, however, never goes away.

Being a Character in the Social Drama

Beyond the more private spheres of self expression, youngsters need to learn how to integrate their inner self with their more public self-expressions in the social drama. Much of traditional school learning focuses on the mastery of the accepted ways of understanding and engaging the world. In this sense schools provide conceptual maps of 'how things work'.[7] These maps comprise the commonly assumed understandings that make up the cultural scenery and staging for the conduct of the social drama. That is to say, they make up the meaning systems, within which the actions of the play is carried out. In one sense those meanings control the whole play, for without them the script is meaningless. One can neither speak one's lines nor understand the lines of the other actors without these cultural meaning systems. Those meaning systems define the character's sense of him or herself, as a person with these rights and these responsibilities, whose public tasks have such and such a meaning, whose work involves a specific constellation of technologies which are understood to work in certain specific ways.

Schools tend to teach this universe of meaning as a given, as describing an ontologically fixed and transparent world. Gravity and energy and light and money and political institutions work *this way*. The social drama then becomes an action that takes place within and around these fixed parts of the landscape and scenery.

Schools, however, could teach that this universe of meaning is a construct or system of constructs humans have devised in their effort to make sense out of the world. These maps help them to govern themselves in ways that promote some kind of social and natural harmony. Schools could continue to socialize youngsters into the conventions of the social drama and to the cultural meaning systems which undergird it. But that socialization need not be so self assured, so dogmatic. It could also point to the common responsibility of everyone in the social drama, including the youngsters themselves, to create, explore or restore alternative responses to make the social drama work better.

Then the social drama can *include* the search for better ways of understanding and engaging in communal self governance as part of what it means to be a character in the social drama. Then the social drama can understand itself as a human construct, a cultural construct by which humans attempt to find individual and collective fulfilment. Then the social drama becomes self reflective, intentional and creative.

From this perspective, being an authentic character in the social drama becomes the only way to play one's part. The social drama and its conventions allow one to continue the project of creating one's character. But that character cannot be created at the expense of other characters in the drama, by deceiving or manipulating them. Neither can that character be created without engaging in the task of bringing new meanings to the drama itself, as it is played out on one's small stage, or as it is played out on the larger stage of one's communal history.

To engage in the social drama from this perspective enables each character to act in authentically heroic ways and to pursue heroic fulfilment (rather than a false heroism embedded in externally manipulated meanings superimposed on conventional behavior). Not only can one be the person one secretly wanted to be, but by being that unique person, one brings new life and new meaning to the social drama. Moreover, that engagement in the drama calls forth the communal search to make the drama more humanly satisfying for everyone. The communal responsibility of everyone to engage in the exploration of new conventions, better dramatic forms and more responsive cultural meaning systems instills the social drama with an heroic quality itself.

Conducting schools in this fashion means forming authentic characters who are engaged not only in mastering the cultural conventions of the drama, but in exploring the limitations and the possibilities of the meaning systems behind those conventions. Obviously, such explorations will take into account the developmental limitations of the youngsters. To paraphrase Jerome Bruner, however, it is possible to teach anything to a child, provided it is presented in formats familiar enough to the child. Nurturing authenticity in youth means teaching them to make conventional meanings their meanings, or to alter them until they are able to use the convention constructively for themselves and others in the social drama as they are experiencing it at that time in their lives. Forming characters means that schools teach the power behind knowing something thoroughly, including knowing the limitations of what is known. That power enables one to engage in the social drama and intentionally to improvise when that is called for by using the knowledge one has mastered in the service of the drama.

From this framework, the drama of schooling again takes on a new depth as the schooling in and for the social drama. If the social drama is itself an heroic enterprise, and playing one's part as an authentic character is the truest form of heroism, then schooling youngsters for engaging the drama at this level becomes itself an heroic participation in the social drama.

Notes

1 For one of the better collections of essays on education for character development in this moral sense, see Kevin Ryan and George McLean (Eds) (1987) *Character Development in Schools and Beyond*, New York, Praeger. For more contentious perspectives, see Edward Wynne's (1982) edition of essays culled from the journal *Character* in his book, *Character Policy*, Washington, DC, University Press of America.
2 Becker, E. (1971) *The Birth and Death of Meaning*, New York, The Free Press.
3 *Ibid.*, p. 76.
4 Piaget, J. (1970) *The Science of Education and the Psychology of the Child*, New York, Orion Press; (1948) *The Moral Judgment of the Child*, Glencoe, IL, The Free Press.
5 Kohlberg, L. (1970) 'Stages of moral development as a basis for moral education', in Beck, C. and Sullivan, E. (Eds) *Moral Education*, Toronto, University of Toronto Press.
6 Erickson, E. (1950) *Childhood and Society*, New York, W. W. Norton.
7 See the delightful and instructive book by David Macaulay (1988) *The Way Things Work*, Boston, Houghton Mifflin Company.

Chapter 6

The Drama of Schooling:
The Formation of a People

The well publicized report, *A Nation at Risk*, alarmed the nation by warning that if a foreign power wanted so to weaken our nation that it would easily succumb to foreign domination, it could do no better than what the schools had been doing for the past several years.[1] The report was referring to the decline of academic achievement in literacy, mathematics and science which, the report maintained, were necessary to maintain America's competitive edge in world economics. That report can be faulted on many grounds (a spurious use of declining achievement scores to excuse decades of poor business decisions by American corporations; a simple-minded linking of schooling to the exclusive interests of Corporate America, etc.), but its primary weakness is its total neglect of the school's responsibility to develop political literacy, political imagination, and political will. The authors of the report simply reflected the political perspective of the dominant party at the time, which indeed saw economic competition and economic productivity as the central political issue.[2]

There is ample evidence to suggest that the solution to the malaise of the nation does not lie in the schools' greater efficiency in preparing workers for the twenty-first century, who will carry on business with the same disregard for the political, social and environmental consequences of their business decisions. That report simply increases the demands of an already flawed policy for schooling but now with more frenetic desperation. As one pundit quipped, 'It is like requiring someone who cannot swim one hundred meters to swim two hundred meters'. One might add that the paradigm upon which that criticism is based is changing; in an increasingly interdependent and endangered world, competition between swimmers is no longer an apt metaphor.

The problem, on the contrary is much deeper. Robert Bellah and his associates sum it up quite well:

> There is a widespread feeling that the promise of the modern era is slipping away from us. A movement of enlightenment and liberation that was to have freed us from superstition and tyranny has led in the twentieth century to a world in which ideological fanaticism and political oppression have reached extremes unknown in previous history. Science, which was to have unlocked the bounties of nature, has given us the power to destroy all life on earth. Progress, modernity's master idea, seems less compelling when it appears that it may be progress into the abyss.[3]

Their study of contemporary Americans indicates a disengagement from public life, a disillusionment with the increasing demands of the work place without a corresponding sense of fulfilment. The study lays bare the schizophrenic separation of work from the private world in which individuals are free to pursue an isolated self fulfilment. The real problem, they conclude, is not economic; it is not even political. The problem is fundamentally moral; it has to do with fundamental meanings by which human striving makes any sense.[4] Without such a basic fabric of meanings, economics and politics drift into propaganda and Madison Avenue fantasy-manipulation. Ultimately, those meanings have to situate individual human striving within a community, within that community's sense of itself, within some sense of common good that simultaneously supports generous levels of self fulfilment.

To be a citizen of a country implies an understanding of much more than the names of major governmental positions and the rules of voting. To be a citizen implies an understanding of that network of meanings that binds people together in political and governing covenants. Those meanings involve very fundamental realities, realities such as one's civil and human rights; agreements about the rights of women, the elderly and the physically and mentally disabled; beliefs about the nature and source of authority; traditions about marriage, education of the young, ownership and inheritance of property — to name some of the more important. That is why, in framing the Declaration of Indepenence, the Constitution and the

Bill of Rights, the founders of the American Republic took great pains to state what those foundational meanings and values were upon which the country would be built and which would undergird the drama of citizens acting together to govern themselves and chart their future. Phrases such as 'We, the People...' and 'We hold these truths...' refer to such foundational agreements and to a sense of being bound in a unity of sentiment and perspective.[5] The schooling for and in that drama of citizenship is inadequate if it does not nurture the understandings and covenants which constitute that network of meanings. On the contrary, when schooling for and in the drama of public life nurtures values and beliefs that weaken those basic understandings and covenants, then indeed the nation is at risk.

The Cynic's Complaint: Schooling for Utopia

The easy way out, of course, is to side with the cynics who claim that this has all been proposed before, to no avail. George Counts' 'Dare the Schools Build A New Social Order?' has already been laughed down the side streets of history. Plato's *Republic*, though studied as a fanciful exercise in philosophy, has never been taken seriously. Educators continue to discuss civic education and citizenship education,[6] even though serious scholars in political science no longer take the notion of citizen seriously.[7] They tend instead to see politics in terms of power, élites, ideology, organization and technique. As citizenship came to be viewed as a matter of subjective choice, an exercise in free will, then citizens were seen by political thinkers more as people controlled and manipulated. Political socialization replaced political education. Through socialization, norms basic to social order were internalized by the people. The vote became the sole exercise of political influence on the state. Democracy became a method to maintain order rather than to create rational politics by which the people might govern themselves.[8]

Such a cynical view does not correspond entirely to the facts, although it is a healthy corrective to naive optimism. In so far as there has been a widespread withdrawal of involvement in civic life, however, as Bellah and others suggest, the crisis in American public life will continue to grow. If the crisis is not addressed, democracy may simply become an outmoded idea.

To be sure, schools cannot dare to build a new social order; they cannot solve the crisis by themselves; they probably are not even the primary agents for restoring democracy. The gradual restoration and growth of a democratic community will require an interlocking effort of many institutions in society. Certainly the school must be one of them.

If public life is indeed a drama, and we believe it unmistakably is, and this drama has indeed become problematical to itself, then the script must be rewritten. The school will not rewrite the script. But the school can rehearse the future actors of this drama in the basic demands of the drama, and the basic arguments about its future. And if the crisis in the public drama is over basic meanings by which human striving takes on value and significance, then the school, traditionally seen as the agency that nurtures the community's tenuous hold on meaning among its young, is the natural place to school the young for dealing with that crisis in the drama. The school performs this function by forming in the young an awareness that they are a people.

What Constitutes A People?

A people comes to be a people over time. Each 'People' comes to be a people through the particular circumstances that make up its history. The French are a people; the Israelis are a people; the Palestinians are a people. The differing perspectives one encounters within each of these peoples derives from their history, and indeed makes up part of the fabric of their unique character as a people. The people of the United States were fashioned in a history that extends from the early colonies of Europeans who came to the new continent seeking religious freedom, to the loose amalgamation of states resisting the Crown, to the contentious forming of a federal government, to the almost continuous tension between the states' authority and the authority of the federal government (a tension galvanized in the civil war), to a more international involvement with other democracies of the West in two world wars, and up to the present global realigning of world powers. Throughout that history, a people was being formed through almost continuous immigration of new ethnic groups, through the movement west as the frontier expanded, through various emancipatory movements of women, slaves, workers, blacks, gays, greys, Hispanics, native Americans and others. Commerce, industry, technology, media and art have all played a part in the history of this people, as have universities, political parties, unions, charitable organizations, religious communities and various charismatic individuals.

Over time a core of belief and values was forged in that history, values which tend to weave themselves into the collective consciousness of this people, values such as enterprise, justice, equality before the law, freedom of speech, of assembly, of religion. These values can be called upon as sources of unity during times of fragmentation or crisis, for they are the basic values the people know were fought over and won at a great price.

A people is united by a common culture. In the United States, that culture is a more loosely woven fabric, due to the many subcultures that make up the people, whereas in England or in France, the people have a more unified sense of their culture. Cultures are made up of folkways, of stories about heroes and villains, of high culture and popular culture, of traditions, art forms, ways of speaking, mythologies. Culture is never static, however. It is always in the process of being made, remade, destroyed, transformed, as people in any given society strive to make meaning and interpret their experience of the drama of life.

A people may also be a polity, a people organized into a political unit, whether that unit be a village, a city, a state or a nation. As we use the term here, we refer to the people as a nation. Scholars of the modern era indicate that a modern nation-state has to develop four capabilities, if it is to maintain its stability. Those four capabilities are: (1) internal political *integration* (a form of social cohesion that goes beyond blood or kinship ties to a national identity); (2) external *accommodation* (through negotiation and compromise, the preservation of mutual security when interacting with other states); (3) *participation* (whereby the people, or a substantial proportion of them, can engage in the formulation of public policy and the renewal of governing structures); (4) *distribution* (by which the economy and social structures respond regularly to demands for the distribution of social and material goods).[9]

A people develops into a people when it sustains the above capabilities. In other words, the drama of public life involves a people attending to its sense of social and cultural identity, to the forms and the substance of political participation, to the ways in which public goods are distributed and to the relationships it establishes with other peoples. The national identity is crucial when major policy decisions must be made, because those national policies have to be based on the good of the people, rather than on the good of an individual, or of a select coterie of the people. While we may wish to retain all of our income, we recognize the need to give over a fair share for the maintenance of roads and highways, hospitals, universities and parks. In time of war, the sense of national identity is called upon to justify the drafting of young people into the military.

Similarly, the distribution of social and material goods enables a people to live with a sense that everyone receives a relatively fair share, whether that involves access to schools, museums, hospitals and parks, money for food and shelter, access to work and housing, etc. People will lend their support to the laws of the state, and will work at their daily tasks, if they believe that the state is attending to the needs of all, rather than using the labor of the many to benefit the few.

Furthermore, if a people enjoys many opportunities to participate in political life, then the state will be seen to be more expressive of their will; the people can more legitimately say, 'This is my country'. Finally, a people needs a sense of their part in the world drama among peoples, even those considered to be enemies. A people cannot be a people in isolation, especially in the twentieth century. Every country must make accommodation for world opinion, to global ecological needs, to a reasonable balance in world economies.

A people derives its identity and its integrity not only from its past, but also from its idealized future. That is to say, a people engages in the drama of its moment of history by being true to the achievements of its past as well as to the promise of its past. The people participate in the drama of history, not only with a sense of who they are, but of who they might be. The integrity of their action involves being true to their traditions, and also true to their dreams.

A people forms a polity in order to institutionalize non-violent means for settling conflicts, for asserting rights and for interpreting and applying the law of the land or of the community. The public drama is taking place on many stages:

* in state and national legislative debates about protecting the environment, about aid to farmers, about responses to the drug epidemic, about nuclear weaponry;

* in neighborhoods where groups argue about zoning, neighborhood schools, the posting of traffic lights, about security against drug trafficking;
* in business where people make decisions about investment, about trying new products, about closing down a plant and laying off 600 workers;
* in service agencies such as a welfare office where a social worker is trying to arrange temporary housing for a homeless mother and her child, or a parole board which is deciding whether to parole a prisoner, or a counselling center where a family counselor listens to a couple talk through their problems.

In all of these scenes, some with seemingly larger social consequences than others, a people is making history, its own history. This people is in the process of governing themselves. In doing so they decide whether to pursue a higher, common good, or to seek only individual interests. In those decisions they remember that they are a people and therefore have responsibilities to one another, or they deny that they are a people and opt for selfish concerns. That is the essence of the public drama of social life. All of that action takes place in settings which political, economic and cultural institutions have scripted, at least with the general rules for the exchange. In a democratic polity, those scripts must always be open to negotiation, must always be flexible enough to allow improvisation in the service of a more humanly fulfilling response to the question being posed, must always take into account the larger good of the community. Are the players totally constrained by the script or can they rewrite the script to make the drama more humanly satisfying? As each individual plays out his or her part, do they have any sense of speaking the lines for the people, of being, in microcosm, the people?

In speaking so hopefully about the people on the journey to peoplehood, it is important to acknowledge that there remain deep feelings of alienation among the people. Such alienation from the state and all its institutions stems partly from the revulsion over the brutalities of two world wars and the suppression of rights by contemporary totalitarian as well as nominally democratic states. Part of that alienation stems simply from the size and complexity of the modern state.[10] Alienation, though almost universal,[11] is felt particularly by segments of the community who have suffered overt and subtle forms of discrimination, not only through the actions of other people, but also through the action of the state itself. As women find a common voice, the smoldering and justifiable anger within that community will begin to surprise many men, who have taken those forms of discrimination and the stereotypes that supported them for granted.[12] It will take a long time for that intense alienation to be healed. Similarly for Blacks and Hispanics and American Indians, their histories of mistreatment at the hands of the majority white population and the American government has left a profound residue of alienation.[13] Despite gains in civil rights legislation, these communities continue to suffer inordinately in the drama of public social life, whether that involves the arena of employment, health care, legal services, or educational opportunities. Schools face a special challenge from those groups in attempting to create a sense of civic participation.

Forming a People

Schools sensitive to the drama of public life can help to form a people. In one sense, schools form a people whether they consciously attempt to or not. They do this by the collective modelling of the teachers, by the informal curriculum of rewards and sanctions, by the values which the institutional structures and processes reflect and by the explicit curriculum.[14]

Schools form a people by teaching the young their history. The history taught, however, must always be related to the present public drama of the people. The history is taught as dramatic, that is as something the people made through concrete choices and actions. This history contains both tragic, heroic and comic elements, just as today's public drama does. As this history is taught, the young are led to understand the values their forebears struggled for, the beliefs about what social life was supposed to mean. This history teaches what the stakes always are in social life: freedom, justice, dignity, honor, loyalty, honesty, as well as the betrayal of those values. This history teaches both the grandeur of the American Revolution as well as the national shame of slavery. This history teaches the lessons of human fallibility, of risk-taking in ambiguous circumstances, of imperfect knowledge, of misguided enthusiasm, of human madness, as well as the examples of heroic striving... all part of a heritage from the past and actively working in the present. This history teaches the original debates over the concrete political expression of various values and principles, debates which are still going on today. This history teaches about the heroes and villains, the popular outlaws and renegades, the mythical characters celebrated in song and stone, in paint and photography which help to define them as a people.

Beyond history, schools which form a people help the young to understand the polity of the people. This involves teaching how the polity is structured, the branches of government, the levels of government, etc. It involves, more importantly, teaching how a people exercises political action. Here, practical lessons in addressing the four functions of the state (national identity, international accommodation, participation and distribution) will help to illustrate how they play a part in the public drama.

The forming of a people involves schooling the young in how to work through conflict to common agreements. The relatively successful settlement of conflict is absolutely essential for a people to have a sense of themselves as a people. Sometimes simulations can enable the young to rehearse a conflictual situation and play it through several times until they hit upon a solution acceptable to all. At other times, situations within the school itself will present both teachers and students with a conflict or a series of conflicts which need to be addressed. Conflictual situations in the school could involve charges of favoritism, unfair grading, arbitrary administrative decisions, as well as disagreements over proper sanctions for certain violations of school rules. Sometimes those conflicts may be racial, religious, class, or cultural.

Schools exhibit ambivalence toward multicultural scripts. Too often American educators, who tend to be white and middle class, think that the school is supposed to bring youngsters from different racial or ethnic backgrounds into the 'mainstream' — that is, into the white, middle class mainstream they inhabit. Granted that employment and political participation involves mastering the basics of the common language used in employment and public discourse, schools have to be sensitive to the family backgrounds and cultural communities of their students. The school is the site where the drama of racial and cultural mixing is negotiated. Instead of suppressing cultural and racial animosities, schools need to deal with the stereotyping and scapegoating those animosities involve.

Multicultural communities are frequently dealing with scripts that prevent them from achieving mutual understanding and respect. Schools need to help them invent new scripts, new language, even, to explore their differences and their commonalities. This will involve very sensitive coaching of the drama, requiring repeated rehearsals of communication in conflicting situations until the players have reached agreements about how to live together with their differences. Beyond that challenge, teachers will have to encourage their multicultural students to stretch beyond their culture to engage in the mainstream drama. That will require a sensitive negotiation of learning what works in the mainstream while maintaining a comfortable sense of one's own cultural integrity.

The School As a Polity

A moment's reflection will lead to the conclusion that for schools to function in this way, they themselves must model what they are trying to teach youngsters. That is to say, schools must intentionally deal with themselves as a polity, with the same challenges any modern state faces in dealing with questions of group identity, participation, distribution and accommodation. Hence, again, the schooling of the drama turns into the drama of schooling. The drama of schooling involves the school engaging itself as a social institution which teaches as much by institutional example as it does by its textbooks. Attention to the continuous, multiple ways of forming a group identity through school songs, mottos, rituals, competitions, assemblies and traditions enables a school to form and sustain a group identity and character. The school engages this group identity when calling for individual students to make sacrifices for the common good of the rest of the students. On the other hand, the school can engage students in practices which undermine this sense of community. The practice of pitting students against one another for scarce grades distributed arbitrarily on a normal curve, and then ranking students according to cumulative grade points nurtures attitudes of a crude Social Darwinism, rather than cooperation and community.[15] The commodification of learning which recent school reforms seem to be stressing tends to reduce students to producers of achievement for some impersonal corporate world, or some unknown evaluation researchers at the State Department of Education.[16]

These practices also influence the distribution system in the school.

Distribution issues occur at several levels. The kind of knowledge being distributed is very much a function of curriculum distinctions and grade placements.

Those who are placed in the advanced or honors classes, have access to certain types and levels of knowledge which are denied to students considered average or slow. The advanced and honors students thereby have access to levels of knowledge which can be traded in for acceptance to high prestige colleges. This arrangement is justified by the meritocratic assumptions school officials make, namely, that everyone has an equal chance to earn the privilege of taking honors or advanced classes, but only some students merit seats in those classes by their actual performance. The assumption of an academic market place of fair competition among roughly equal competitors is simply unfounded.[17]

Even if one were to concede the meritocratic arrangement, what about the common core of knowledge necessary for all the students to function in the drama of the real world? In elementary schools serving the urban poor, that content has been defined as minimum competency in language and numeracy. That definition, in turn, is tied to an almost exclusively vocational (economic) interpretation of schooling, namely to prepare youngsters for the workplace. Urban high schools serving that same population are tending more and more toward a system of magnet schools, specializing in areas, again, more directly related to vocational concerns, with a few select schools reserved for the high academic achievers who have a chance at a prestige university. In such school systems, education for citizenship and community building is mentioned, if at all, as a kind of afterthought.

How does the school structure participation? How do students have some say in areas of legitimate concern to them? The traditional student government tends not to engage students beyond the level of a popularity contest, because there are no areas of school life which student government truly controls. Similarly, parents have few institutional structures for participating in school life. Their presence adds to the problematics of group identity, but not hopelessly so. A further question might be asked. What exactly is the nature of the political life of the school in which one might want to participate? Does it extend to the choice of textbooks, and books for the library, and the class schedule and grading criteria? These are difficult questions, but unless the school creates greater opportunities for genuine participation, then the familiar sense of alienation toward school will continue to pervade the student culture.

The issue of boundaries and accommodation to those communities which lie outside the polity of the school appears to stretch the analogy with the polity of the nation-state too far, for the school lies within the nation-state and is an agency of that state. Nonetheless, the school as a cultural institution has an integrity of its own, and that integrity will always place it in tension with its sponsor, the public. In reality, the school always has to negotiate its boundaries with the outside community, whether the people from the community be the Chamber of Commerce, military recruiters, or religious proselytizers.

A People Empowered

The formation of a people involves not only developing an identity which provides direction to their drama, but it also involves empowering them to govern themselves. Empowerment comes from knowledge, but not simply from knowledge of the facts. Empowering knowledge is the knowledge of how to do something. What is all too often missing in the school reform recommendations is concern for this kind of empowerment. Rather, the schooling being recommended is mastery of basic skills in order to be able to follow directions, or at best to understand how complex systems someone else has designed work, so one can operate them. All too often schools encourage a passive mastery of knowledge. One is assumed to have mastered knowledge when one can pass a test on that material. There are very few tests which present a problem to be found in the real world and ask students to generate alternative solutions to them, detailing the probable consequences of various choices.

The way one is taught to appropriate knowledge is a political act. Teachers who present youngsters with a script to be memorized, not a script to be improvised, are preparing their students for political passivity. Teachers who constantly stress the value of knowledge for its usefulness in participating in the human drama are teaching their students how to participate more fully in the drama. Teaching the passive acceptance of knowledge teaches a way of looking at the world. Teaching the active application of knowledge to human problems is teaching the responsibilities of citizenship. It is empowering youth to employ their knowledge in the service of the human community.

Schooling enables us to reduce the scale of the drama in the public realm to readable scripts and plots. Textbooks replay the drama in consumable simplicity, but do not encourage experimentation with alternative scripts and sets. In schools that empower their students for active participation in the social drama, students read the script of the public drama critically; they look at the political economy of the drama; they examine the politics implied in the proposed metaphysics of relationships between humans, or between humans and nature, or between humans and large organizations; they analyze the politics of the language of the script itself. The knowledge derived from that critical reading of the script is empowering. From that knowledge they can rehearse alternatives to the present forms of the social drama.

Notes

1 The National Commission on Excellence in Education (1983) *A Nation At Risk: The Imperative for Educational Reform*, Washington, DC, United States Department of Education.

2 The authors of the report can hardly be singled out for a failing that has permeated the thinking and the policies of educators and government officials for generations. For criticisms of such failings see the following sample of authors: Pratte, R. (1988) *The Civic Imperative: Examining the Need for Civic Education*, New York, Teachers College Press; Finklestein, B. (1985) 'Thinking publicly about civic learning: An agenda for education reform in the '80s', in Jones, A. (Ed.) *Civic Learning for Teachers: Capstone for Educational Reform*, Ann Arbor, MI, Prakken Publications, pp. 13–24; Giroux, H. (1984) 'Public philosophy and the crisis in education', *Harvard Educational Review*, 54, 2, pp. 186–194; Becker, E. (1967) *Beyond Alienation: A Philosophy of Education for the Crisis of Democracy*, New York, George Braziller.

3 Bellah, R., Madsen, R., Sullivan, W., Swidler, A., and Tipton, S., (1985) *Habits of the Heart: Individualism and Commitment in American Life*, New York, Harper and Row, p. 277.

4 *Ibid.*, p. 295.

5 Samuel Huntington reveals that the American Constitution and Bill of Rights are grounded in an older English tradition of natural law derived more from

Tudor England and its medieval roots, than from the modern British and European rationalization of authority and public law. See Huntington, S. (1966) 'Political modernization: America vs. Europe', *World Politics*, 18, 3, pp. 378–414.

6 See Wynne, E. (1982) 'Citizenship education: The state of the art', in Wynne, E. (Ed.) *Character Policy*, Washington, DC, University Press of America, pp. 77–78; also, Pratte, R. (1988) *op. cit.*

7 See Herman van Gunsteren's exploratory essay (1978) 'Notes on a theory of citizenship', in Birnbaum, P., Lively, J. and Parry, G., (Eds) *Democracy, Consensus and Social Contract*, Beverly Hills, CA, Sage Publications, pp. 9–35.

8 *Ibid.*, pp. 18–21.

9 Almond, G. (1963) 'Political Systems and Political Change', *American Behavioral Scientist*, 6, 6, pp. 3–10.

10 See Eisenstadt's commentary on Weber's notion of alienation which, unlike Marx, placed alienation as a common experience within modern society in *all* (not simply economic) social arrangements: Eisenstadt, S. (1968) *Max Weber: On Charisma and Institution Building*, Chicago, University of Chicago Press, pp. xv–xvii.

11 For insightful essays on sources of alienation in the modern state see the collection contained in *Daedalus*, 108, 4, (1979, Fall).

12 See Clarke, M. and Lange, L. (1979) (Eds) *The Sexism of Social and Political Theory: Women and Reproduction from Plato to Nietszche*, Toronto, University of Toronto Press.

13 See the collection of essays in *Daedalus*, 110, 2 (1981, Spring).

14 See Pratte, R. (1988) *op. cit.*, for some fresh challenges to the schools, despite its political naiveté. Pratte senses, as do others, that the issue confronting modern democratic societies over citizenship involves a lack of consensus over political theory. He challenges the schools to face the theory issue.

15 See Lesko, N. (1988) *Symbolizing Society*, Methuen NJ, Falmer Press, for a good case study on this point.

16 Wexler, P. (1987) *Social Analysis of Education: After the New Sociology*, London, Routledge and Kegan Paul.

17 See, for example, the following: Bellah *et al.*, (1985) *op. cit.*, p. 208; Coleman, J. (1966) *Equality of Educational Opportunity*, Washington, DC, Government Printing Office; Carnoy, M. and Levin, H., (1985) *Schooling and Work in the Democratic State*, Stanford, CA, Stanford University Press.

Chapter 7

Reflective Practice as Dramatic Consciousness

Awareness of the drama of schooling involves teaching with dramatic consciousness. Although that understanding of teaching has been implied all along, it will be helpful to develop that understanding more fully. Dramatic consciousness means being aware that there is dramatic action taking place in one's life, in one's work, in the lives of the people who make up the school community. It implies being present to that drama, engaged in its passions, struggles and adventures, rather than being psychologically distant, removed from the action.

Dramatic consciousness can be contrasted to bureaucratically anaesthetized consciousness. One can go through the work day with a minimum of presence to people and to the details of work. The work can be highly structured and organized, hence highly predictable. The demands of the work may be relatively superficial, such as taking readings from meters, delivering mail, running an elevator, or packing cans in a supermarket. In these circumstances, the work does not take a great deal of concentration. It does not require attention to complex relationships between variables in a constant state of flux. Furthermore, the work does not deal with subtleties of meaning, carefully nuanced communications, actions carrying weighty consequences. One can attend minimally to what one is doing in these circumstances while simultaneously carrying on an imaginary conversation with one's lover, reliving the excitement of last night's cinema, or imagining a more creative execution of one's mother-in-law.

Dramatic consciousness involves a gathering up of the loose edges of one's attention to a concentrated focus on what one is doing or witnessing.

That concentration is driven by a feeling of significance and importance to the moment. The moment is pregnant for the people involved. It can blossom into insight, break forth into surprise, transform anger into acceptance, guide agitation into quiet. Any episode can mean a moving forward or a falling backward; a victory or a defeat; a breaking loose from unhealthy bonds, or another surrender to them; an acceptance of a challenge; or a retreat from risk; an act of heroism, or an act of cowardice. The advance, victory, or act of heroism does not have to be of cosmic proportions; it may be a matter of inches in a person's growth. Normally, that is how it is with most people: tiny victories, mini-disclosures, small risks, micro-insights, miniature spontaneities, minor miracles. Those are the stuff of the everyday human drama. The teacher with that sense of dramatic consciousness knows, however, that with youngsters, those inch-long choices, those atoms of understandings, those grams of achievement — when continually nurtured — lead to life-long patterns of human growth and fulfilment, not simply for the individual, but for the human community as well.

Reflective Practice

Recently the work of Donald Schon has highlighted a problem in the professions, including the profession of teaching.[1] His research among professional doctors, lawyers, engineers, architects and administrators indicates that the long-assumed paradigm of professional education is mistaken. That paradigm was based on the belief that if one went to university and learned the theory behind one's profession, one would be able upon graduation to practice the profession by applying the theory to the problems one encountered in one's practice. As a matter of fact, none of the professionals Schon encountered followed the paradigm. None of them explicitly thought very much about the theory they had learned in university. All of them responsed to the problems and projects in their practice with hunches, guesses and intuitions based on the trial and error learning from their past experience.

The problem, apparently, is that reality does not conform to theory.[2] Patients, for example, never come to a doctor's office with a problem corresponding to the 'model problem' of the textbooks. Their medical problem is usually complicated by age, sex, influence of other physical ailments and medications being taken for them, occupation, family stress, parent and sibling medical histories, etc. Doctors tend to rely on their experience, rummaging about in their memory for cases that resemble the present one. They then apply a treatment that seemed to work for those symptoms.

Similarly, engineers have to deal with problems which the theory does not cover. Each problem has a host of variables which need to be figured into the possible solution, variables such as temperature, climate, erosion, moisture, wind, properties of various materials under various conditions, stress limits under extreme conditions, budget projections, environmental regulations, etc. They, too, rely on their past experience to provide hunches about the best response to the problem. The addition of computerized simulations has enabled engineers to try out these hunches before committing to a course of action.

Schon's work and others' have led to the understanding that reflection is at the heart of effective practice.[3] Practitioners who spend time thinking about the results of their actions, who puzzle out why things work and why they do not work, tend to build up a reservoir of insights and intuitions which they can call upon as they go about their work. Not only do they reflect after the fact, but they can bring this reflective frame of mind to the problem at hand. They are reflecting even in the moment of action so they can respond to the action as it unfolds.

Theory enters into this reflection in action only as offering a possible explanation, and usually as a *partial* explanation of the causes of or contributors to the problem at hand. In other words, theory provides frames or lenses by which one can analyze and explore a problem or situation; they sometimes help to illuminate and provide conceptual lineaments to one's intuition. Theory, however, sometimes blocks insight into other possible explanations of and solutions to the problem. Because theory structures or organizes experience according to a limited number of controlling concepts, it tends to blind the theorizer to phenomena that fall outside those conceptual frames.

Responsive Teaching as Reflective Practice

Sergiovanni likens teaching to surfing.[4] The surfer has to respond to every nuance of the surge of the wave; so, too, the teacher must try to be responsive to the ripples of energy, curiosity and insight in the classroom. There can never be a one-to-one correspondence between an identified 'learning outcome' and a teaching strategy or protocol. Most good teachers will have four or five ways to represent the point they want the students to learn.[5] Different representations are necessary because some will make more sense to some students than to others. Students who come from different backgrounds will use that background experience to make sense out of the curriculum unit they confront that day in class. Depending on what has preceded that unit and what will follow, one or two treatments by the teacher may be more appropriate than another. As surfers sense the wind, the height and speed of the wave, the disposition of their weight and position on the board, and use instant calculations to adjust and stabilize their position on the wave, so too the responsive teacher makes countless instantaneous readings of what is happening to the students so as to adjust the class activity to that movement among the students. Sergiovanni's metaphor captures the essence of responsive teaching. It also exemplifies reflective practice. Instead of mechanically following the lesson plan, the teacher is present to the ebb and flow of questions, silences, body language within the class and adjusts the pace and stimuli to maintain engagement with the students' energy and interest.

The metaphor of surfing translates easily, in our discussion of the drama of schooling, as improvisation. The instantaneous adjustments are improvisations in the dramatic action of a classroom full of youngsters caught up in the excitement of learning. By looking at the practice of teaching as disciplined improvisation, we can perhaps understand how dramatic consciousness aids reflective practice.

'Reflective practice' can be all too easy a generalization, however. We need some examples of how reflection enters into the flow of practice. Three instances of reflection illustrate their influence on practice: reflection as problem naming; reflection as intentional use of one's educational platform; reflection as double loop learning.

Problem Naming

Studies of decision making and problem solving have indicated that the critical factor in good decision making and problem solving is the naming of the problem.[6] Some use the term problem finding, or problem setting; problem naming is to be preferred because of its accent on naming, which implies both conceptualizing as well as imagining.

When the problem is incorrectly named, the solution is usually inappropriate and ineffective. Sometimes a problem is seen differently by different people. A student is sent to the principal's office for repeatedly failing to do her homework. The problem could be called disobedience; it could be called laziness; it could be called having no place at home to do homework; it could be called a learning disability not previously diagnosed; it could be called an ineffective teacher; the problem might be child abuse at home, parental quarrels, or whatever. We cannot helpfully respond to the student until we have identified and named what the real problem is.

Schon suggests that generative metaphors contained in stories people tell about problems are a key to understanding how they name the problem.[7] His analysis suggests a group discussion of the problem, such that the group characterizes the problem in common metaphorical terms. Kolb similarly emphasizes a group discussion of the nature of the problem, relating the identification of the problem to the organization's goals and priorities.[8] In other words, problem naming involves relating the situation to values and purposes; the problem is a problem precisely insofar as it interferes with people's goals.

This suggests that teachers, in their attempt to be responsive to their students, constantly have to explore with the student what it is that prevents the youngster from learning. Furthermore, it suggests that the teacher discuss the nature of the problem with the student or students who are experiencing the problem. The students' experience of the problem will probably be expressed in narrative. Within the narrative, teachers can look for those images and metaphors which may enable them to give a name to the problem. Only when the participants in the problem agree about what the problem really is can they explore an appropriate solution. By establishing patterns of reflective problem-naming with students, teachers are also coaching them to become reflective practitioners in their own right. Furthermore, when students are involved in naming the problem, they will tend to take more responsibility for trying solutions. Again, through this process teachers are coaching students to become actors in the drama, rather than patients in a clinic.

When we think about the word 'reflective', we recognize that it means to re-flex, that is to bend back upon. In problem-naming we try to look back over the problem to see it in its context, to see it as part of a larger whole, or to see it is a part of a pattern. When we name the problem, we abstract from the immediacy of the details of the problem and see it in its structural aspects, that is as fitting one or more categories or images by which we can analyze its basic meaning. So we ask, 'Is this a political problem, an emotional problem, a definitional problem, a resource problem, a goal-conflict problem, an identity problem, etc.?' Sometimes we may not be able to name the problem clearly, nor to identify it as one among several potential names. It may, in fact, be a false problem. Normally the best response is to let the problem emerge to the point where it can be identified, or to the point where it appears as a false problem.

As Schon indicates, our experience will aid us considerably in our efforts to name problems accurately. Most on-the-job learning involves trial and error. Error can be a great teacher. When we see a problem that we tried to solve in a certain way in the past and remember that our solution blew up in our face, that experience will cause us to be cautious about trying that solution again. It may also lead us to consider whether we had named the problem correctly.

In the practice of problem-naming, teachers are frequently helped by engaging other teachers in the effort to name the problem. The collective experience and hence the collective practical wisdom of others can far surpass what we individually are able to bring to the naming of a problem. That collective wisdom can also generate a larger variety of possible responses to the problem than an individual teacher.

Educational Platform

A second example of reflective practice is the intentional use of one's educational platform on an everyday basis in the classroom.[9] Political parties have what they call a platform. The elements of a platform, often called 'planks', indicate those fundamental beliefs and values which will guide the decisions of the party while they hold office. Platforms can also be statements of priorities or significant goals the party wants to achieve. A teacher's educational platform is something like that. Beneath the observable 'bag of tricks' every teacher brings into the classroom, there is a floor of beliefs, opinions, values and attitudes which influence the way teachers behave and make decisions in their work. That platform includes beliefs about the way children develop, about the nature of learning, about the relationship between schooling and adult life in society. Platforms also include opinions about the balance between discipline and creativity, between conformity to rules and personal autonomy, between social and academic learning, between required and enrichment learnings, etc.

Platforms are usually not expressed in formal statements. They are usually unspoken assumptions, truisms that seem so obvious they do not need to be voiced. An element of a platform will emerge frequently in response to a friendly question, 'Why did you do such and so in that class?' The response will come out something like, 'Well, you see, children at this age need very clear instruction when we approach a homework assignment'. Embedded in this statement are assumptions about their children's cognitive development and motivation, as well as the efficacy of structuring a learning episode. Another teacher might respond, 'Well, you see, children at this age have a natural sense of curiosity and phantasy. That's why I build up a sense of mystery about the homework assignment. It's like saying, "Who can find the buried treasure?" or "Who will free the princess from the enchanted castle by discovering the magic formula?" We keep it close to their imaginative world'. That teacher reveals elements of quite a different platform, assumptions about the role of imagination in leading and structuring learning, about motivation, and about encouraging children to find answers by puzzling through an assignment.

Because teachers often act on these disciplined institutions without ever questioning their validity, it frequently helps to make the platform explicit. Although teachers normally find it a very difficult exercise at first, writing out their platform forces them to reflect on the beliefs that ground their practice. Seeing their platform externalized, they can ask themselves if it may be too narrow, or too one-sided, or inconsistent. That kind of analysis is usually helped considerably by reviewing the platform with another teacher.

Each teacher's platform will be unique, both in its form and in its substance. Some are very plain and direct; others are more poetic; others are expressed more in visual imagery, such as diagrams or photographs. Because it is an unfamiliar exercise, most find it difficult to get started. However it is expressed, a platform usually contains from five to ten propositions or principles, arranged in different sequences and with different values. Sometimes a platform can be quite simple, containing only two or three 'planks'.

Often these platforms are expressed in statements like the following: (1) The three most important aims of education for youngsters in our school are . . . ; (2) Students usually learn best when . . . : (3) The social significance of what my students learn is . . . ; (4) The most valuable elements of my courses are . . . ; (5) A teacher is . . . ; (6) The best kind of teaching is . . . ; (7) Classroom learning ought to emphasize . . . ; (8) Our school climate should be . . . ; (9) The best kind of student–teacher relationship is . . . ; (10) The overall purpose of my teaching is . . . .

Once the platform is written out, discussed with other teachers, and refined again, some teachers find it helpful to post copies of their platform in their work areas to serve as reminders. Being reminded of one's platform aids reflection on how well one is actually putting the platform into action. As an aid to that reflection, some teachers will use the platform as the starting point for a supervisory cycle with their department chair, or with a peer coach.

Often, however, teachers do not put their platforms into practice. Although they may say, for example, that they believe one of the important learnings they attend to is democratic discussion, they may in reality conduct their classes in very undemocratic ways. With such a teacher, there are two platforms in competition with each other, the platform which the teacher espouses and the actual platform in use.[10] Normally, a teacher is not aware of the disparity between platforms; the teacher is a poor critic of his or her performance.[11] Generally, it will take someone observing a teacher to recognize the discrepancies between the espoused platform and the platform in use — the espoused script and the script in use. This kind of stimulus to reflection will frequently emerge in a peer coaching situation, where self critical insights can more readily emerge in the absence of distractions caused by administrative judgements.[12] Sometimes having one's class videotaped will enable teachers to see the discrepancy. These sometimes jolting experiences ('Do I look *that* bad in the classroom!') introduce the necessary cognitive dissonance for confronting the practice and bringing it more into line with one's espoused platform.[13] Such self confrontation appears to be aided greatly by another observer who can call attention to the teaching behaviors out of line with the espoused platform.[14]

Double Loop Learning

Another example of reflective practice is what Argyris calls double loop learning.[15] Double loop learning is contrasted with single loop learning. In single loop learning, one takes the measure of a situation or a problem, takes action, and then evaluates whether the action led to the expected result. If the action achieved its desired effect, then single loop learning stops there. If the desired effect did not occur, then the single loop learner tries another course of action, and evaluates the result. The double loop learner, on the other hand, seeks to understand why certain actions work and why others do not. Single loop learners are satisfied to know *that* certain actions work; double loop learners try to find out *why*. Double loop learners re-flect, bend back upon the situation and study what is happening, looking at the structural properties and the underlying dynamics of the situation. Hence double loop learners tend to be aware of multiple levels of activity and sensitivity going on beneath the surface. They can utilize multiple perspectives on the situation or problem.

A double loop learner, for example, will recognize that a troublesome boy in her classroom may not be simply a mean and nasty lout. He may be acting that way, because he is considered by his peers to be their leader, and has to stand up to the authority of the teacher to maintain his own status with the group. Thus, the drama requires careful scripting. Recognizing that a simple punitive response will probably result in escalating the battle, the teacher seeks to respond in ways that allow both sides to win. Often the teacher will put the boy in charge of taking attendance, or getting supplies, or some such thing, which allows him to retain his status in the group, and allows her to get on with the class.

A department chair may have to confront a weak, second year teacher whose evaluation reports at the end of her first year were unfavorable. As a double loop learner who reflects upon the professional and bureaucratic dynamics of the drama, the chair would recognize that last year's department chair was incapable of coaching beginning teachers, which left this teacher with no professional support during her first year; the chair also knows that the local teacher union leadership is watching this case closely because of recent dismissals of beginning teachers. The chairperson knows that she wants to help this teacher; she also knows that future cooperation between the union leadership and the school administration may hinge on her careful handling of this teacher. The chair is also aware of her own feelings, that she needs to win this one. These feelings also caution her to balance her need to be fair and helpful with her responsibility to the children to weed out incompetent teachers. The chair, then, is able to reflect on various levels of significance embedded in this drama with this second year teacher. Somehow she must improvise a solution in which everyone wins: the second year teacher, the children, the union and herself.

Both examples point to the efficacy of double loop learning. By keeping in mind the various structural relationships in situations (what's at stake for the various parties involved), double loop learners try to keep situations from degenerating into win-lose battles. Frequently, double loop learners recognize that they appear torn between conflicting principles, such as enhancing students' education by keeping order in the classroom, and helping the wayward student find appropriate ways to maintain enough self esteem to keep trying. Often such apparent conflicts between principles is illusory; honoring both principles frequently points the way to win-win solutions. Double loop learners often look at themselves more critically, as being potentially part of the problem, either by being too defensive, or by holding too narrow a perspective on the situation.

Integrating the Three Examples of Reflective Practice

Each of the three examples illustrates how reflection contributes to the practitioner's ability to make sense out of the challenges and situations he or she faces on the job. Each example of reflective practice points to ways of making meaning, ways of understanding, ways of being present to people and situations. Problem-naming renders the problem intelligible; the platform enables one to follow consistent values while dealing with a parade of characters demanding attention; double loop learning enables one to attend to one's platform and to the multiform levels of meaning to be found in most encounters in the drama of schooling. All three individually are examples of reflective practice; when linked together in consistent patterns of reflective practice, a richer appreciation of the profession of teaching emerges.

Reflection as Dramatic Consciousness

Dramatic consciousness in teaching implies awareness of at least three levels of drama in the school setting: the drama of the individual youngster, the drama of everyday school life and the drama of the world outside the school. There is, first of all, the drama of each young person struggling to find her or himself. For each child that drama has an immediacy to it that dominates all other dramatic involvements. For some children, finding oneself is equated with pleasing the teacher and parents by succeeding at school work. For others, the home situation may be so diffuse, conflicted and confusing that it saps all their energy, leaving them incapacitated to engage in the school drama. For others, coming from secure families, school life may be too dull and uninteresting to hold their attention; sports, music, an after-school job, or some all-consuming hobby may appear far more attractive an arena for self-assertion.

Within these large patterns there are the smaller ups and downs of everyday life whose significance for youngsters takes on enormous weight: the anxiety of trying out for a team, the elation of being chosen for the chorus, the joy of a family picnic, the depression over a pet dying, the total absorption of a stamp collection, the humiliation of having a classmate make fun of one's clothes, the embarrassment of being caught copying someone's homework, discouragement over failing a test, elation at making a friend. In all of these and countless other experiences, youngsters are learning life's lessons, by engaging in life's experiences, by retreating from them, or by learning to manipulate and control them. They are creating themselves more than they are being molded by outside forces. They are learning how to be a somebody — at least in their own eyes. They are making a life for themselves — for better or for worse.

Teachers are aware, more or less, that this is going on in the everyday lives of their children. Some teachers choose to become players in this drama, going beyond the normal classroom role to one who listens after school, suggests outside projects which can channel some of the diffuse energy, makes a call to parents to suggest they talk with their child about a problem the child is having. Some teachers integrate creative and captivating learning experiences with the everyday lives of their students, activities which accomplish the more formal school objectives, while also stimulating life lessons for the individual growth of their students. These teachers recognize that they can be significant players in the life of dramas of their children, not in an exaggerated messianic sense, but simply as friendly encouragers of the potentials youngsters already possess.

Then there is the school drama. As we have seen earlier, this drama can be threatening and confusing to youngsters. It tends to appear as a drama they are forced into, in a theater foreign to their interests and sensibilities, where adults control the costumes, scripts, sets, pacing and criticism of the play. Probably most youngsters would not participate, if given a choice. They would rather be outside exploring the neighborhood or the nearby parks and woods; playing the myriad games of marbles, skip-rope, stick ball, trading cards, hop-scotch; talking over life by telling stories to one another; creating small one act plays of their own with space invaders, or other imaginary characters (assuming they had not been addicted to television in early childhood).

Instead, youngsters are given school roles to play, textbooks as scripts, school clothing to wear, respectful lines to address teachers and administrators, schedules for various activities, rules to follow. For reasons they cannot fathom, enormous importance is placed on their good performance in their studies. They learn early on how to succeed in or frustrate the school drama. As we saw earlier, there is an academic script and a bureaucratic script. Often, these scripts are in conflict, though it is not openly acknowledged.[16]

Teachers who appreciate the constricting nature of the school drama for youngsters, can help them to come to terms with the relentless demands of the drama of schooling while leading them beyond the bureaucratic script to a rich experience of the adventures of the mind and imagination which the academic script can afford. In other words, teachers can bring their youngsters beyond the kind of functional rationality of learning how to get grades and how to get promoted, by using the information they acquire in their courses, to the more profound engagement with the knowledge of the world contained in the academic disciplines of the humanities and the sciences and the arts. The bureaucratic script need not dominate the drama of schooling; the excitement and wonder of knowing the world in all its fascinating complexity and harmony and pathos and promise can instead make schooling truly dramatic. That is the drama of the human mind being instructed, shaped, delighted, enchanted and stretched by the focused engagement with the world.

Consciousness of the drama of the world itself, brings teachers to an even deeper engagement with their students, for it is here that they bring their awareness of the drama of the individual and the drama of the beauty, truth and goodness (despite its flawed human history) of the world into a larger synthetic sense of the drama of our present history and its immediate future. That larger drama is played out on many levels, all of them interdependent on each other, levels that include the political, cultural, economic, religious, social and anthropological.

That drama takes place on a local, national and international scale. It is the drama of the preservation of the biosphere against the accumulation of decades of poisonous assaults; it is the drama of choices for or against nuclear holocaust; it is the drama of regional peace or continuing carnage among groups and small countries armed by the superpowers; it is the drama of integrating national economies into an international economy which respects a fair distribution of the earth's resources; it is the drama of urban communities learning how to tame neighborhood violence; it is the drama of modern technology which has the potential to facilitate global learning networks and global governing networks; it is the drama of rescuing the humanity of the rich and the poor alike, the one exhausted by the struggle to survive, the other emptied of purpose by a gluttony of consumption, so that they might live in some form of human community; it is the drama of mobilizing individual and collective will to bring the human resources of creativity, intelligence, humor and compassion to these and many other basic challenges to our collective human survival.

Teachers with that sense of the drama inherent in the present moment of human history can offer to the youngsters they teach the challenge to find themselves in involvement with this larger drama. They can point to the very knowledge schools have at their disposal as the vehicle of that involvement. But that knowledge in its present scripted form will have to be rescripted, both by teachers and students, so as to engender active forms of learning. Knowledge gained in school cannot be disinterested knowledge, simply something digested and repeated for passing exams and satisfying the strange compulsion of some national spokespeople to have our scores look better than those of our international competitors. Knowledge gained in school must be appropriated and appreciated as part of the effort of the mind and imagination of the educating community to engage in the drama of this moment of history.

Knowledge, then, its discovery and use to make history, comes to be seen not as a prepackaged byte of information, but as the improvisation of the human mind in its effort to engage in the drama of the world. Knowledge is one of the ingredients of the script, but our active use of it on the large stage of public involvement creates history, makes the drama of the world into a human drama, creates new possibilities for human life. Learning the drama and learning how to improve the drama can then be seen as a proleptic act of citizenship. Schooling the drama can likewise be seen as one of the highest forms of citizenship.

In this perspective, learning for individual fulfilment, if it is only for private, personal fulfilment, is seen as too narrow a view of the drama of schooling, and ultimately self-defeating. Learning for grades, higher test scores, placement into a predetermined, competitive, corporate role is similarly seen as too one-dimensional a view of the drama of schooling and similarly self-defeating.

When the drama of schooling involves schooling in the larger drama of the historical moment with all of its enormous challenges, then it offers an adventurous arena for self fulfilment, and opportunities for many satisfying careers and life work. In other words, the drama of individual fulfilment, while enjoying necessary space for its private and personal expression, is enriched and completed by some participation in the larger social drama. Similarly, the drama of schooling as the acquisition of knowledge, while enjoying a necessary autonomy and distance from the hurly burly of the larger drama, nevertheless is enriched and completed by its continuous reference to the larger social drama, and can attend to an appropriate nurturing of the individual drama in the light of this larger social drama.

Reflective Practice as Dramatic Consciousness

Seen from this perspective, the elements of reflective practice discussed earlier take on additional depth and complexity. Problem-naming is facilitated when one can identify some of the problems children and teachers encounter in everyday life in schools as taking place within the individual drama, the school drama, or the larger social drama, or in the interstices of those dramas. Sometimes the problem can be interpreted as a conflict between the bureaucratic and the academic scripts, or within the script itself. Sometimes the problem will be seen as a tension between the roles teachers assume as players, coaches or critics. Sometimes the problem will be named as the inappropriate intrusion of the larger social drama in the form of propaganda or political patronage; at other times the problem will be seen as the larger social drama resisting any critical analyses of the way the drama is conducted, thus frustrating the authentic schooling in the drama of a democratic community.

The way one frames one's educational platform will reflect how one perceives the drama of schooling. Given the point of view expressed here, namely, that dramatic consciousness includes awareness of all three levels of the drama, educational platforms may not take adequate account of all three levels of the drama. Assuming that one was trying to keep one's espoused platform close to one's practice, then the reflective practice of dramatic consciousness would be expressed in a more constant, intentional integration of the three levels of the drama. The drama of schooling would become the schooling of drama.

Finally, the practice of double loop learning within dramatic consciousness would enable teachers to integrate their role as player, coach and critic. As a coach of the drama, the teacher would re-flect (either forward or backward) on the teaching episode to clarify what level of drama was being dealt with, how well the script was working, whether more improvisation was called for, how many runs of the scene might be necessary for the players to master the scene, etc. As a critic, the teacher would not only reflect on the students' performance of the scene, but on his own coaching of the scene. The teacher as critic may decide that the scene needs to be rescripted and rehearsed for a better outcome. The teacher as critic may realize that the bureaucratic script was smothering the academic script, or that the academic script was not sufficiently related to the larger social drama. All of these judgements might lead to a re-run of the lesson so that the dramatic content might be more fully revealed.

In reflecting on the playing out of the classroom drama, the teacher can test whether the lesson is sufficiently responsive to the individual drama, the school drama and the larger public drama. One should not win at the expense of the other; rather, it is by the skilful integration of all three levels of the drama that the demands of all three can best be satisfied. The teacher as critic then goes back to being the coach and works with the players on rescripting the scene and rehearsing it. The purpose of this re-run, of course, is to have the players understand the drama involved, and learn how to improvise in similar circumstances to make the drama work better. In thus enacting the role of coach and critic, the teacher becomes an actor in the drama of schooling. The teacher as a player in the drama of schooling improvises on the script to call attention to the other players that the drama can be made to come out better for everyone. Thus the teacher is inside the drama. The completion of the teacher's self fulfilment also lies in engagement with the public drama, which is the drama of schooling as the schooling of drama.

Notes

1 Schon, D. (1983) *The Reflective Practitioner: How Professionals Think and Act*, New York, Basic Books.
2 For a more detailed development and application to the practice of teachers, see Sergiovanni, T. and Starratt, R. (1988) *Supervision: Human Perspectives*, 4th ed., New York, McGraw-Hill Publishers, pp. 315–319, 331–348.
3 See, for example, Scheffler, I., (1973) *Reason and Teaching*, New York, Bobbs-Merril, p. 185.
4 Sergiovanni and Starratt (1988) *op. cit.*, p. 311.
5 A penetrating analysis of this aspect of teaching is found in Lee Schulman's paper (1989) 'An end to substance abuse: Reclaiming the content for teacher education and supervision', a paper presented at the Annual Meeting of the American Educational Research Association, San Francisco.
6 Shapiro, J. and McPherson, B., (1987) 'State Board desegregation policy: An application of the problem-finding model of policy analysis', *Educational Administration Quarterly*, 23, 2, pp. 60–77; Immegart, G. and Boyd, W. (Eds) (1979) *Problem Finding in Educational Administration*, Lexington, MA, D.C. Heath; Schon, D. (1979) 'Generative metaphor: A perspective on problem-setting in social policy', in Ortony, A., *Metaphor and Thought*, Cambridge, Cambridge University Press.
7 Schon, D. (1979) *op. cit.*, pp. 268–269.

8 Kolb, D. (1983) 'Problem management: Learning from experience', in Scrivasta, S. (Ed.) *The Executive Mind*, San Francisco, Jossey-Bass.

9 For an extended treatment of the concept of educational platform, see Sergiovanni and Starratt (1988) *op. cit.*, pp. 233–245; see also the originator of the concept, Decker Walker (1971) 'A naturalistic model for curriculum development', *The School Review*, 80, 1.

10 See Argyris, C. and Schon, D. (1974) *Theory in Practice: Increasing Professional Effectiveness*, San Francisco, Jossey-Bass.

11 See Lortie, D. (1975) *Schoolteacher: A Sociological Study*, Chicago, University of Chicago Press; Lieberman, A. and Miller, L. (1984) *Teachers, Their World and Their Work*, Alexandria, VA, Association for Curriculum and Curriculum Development.

12 See, for example, Garmston, R. (1988, August) 'A call for collegial coaching', *The Developer*, pp. 1–6; Brandt, R. (1987) 'On teachers coaching teachers; A conversation with Bruce Joyce', *Educational Leadership*, 44, 5, pp. 12–17; Leggett, D. and Hoyle, S. (1987) 'Peer coaching: One district's experience in using teachers as staff developers', *Journal of Staff Development*, 8, 1, pp. 16–20.

13 Moffet, K., St. John, J. and Isken, J. (1987) 'Training and coaching beginning teachers: An antidote to reality shock', *Educational Leadership*, 44, 5, pp. 34–36.

14 Rogers, S. (1987) 'If I can see myself, I can change', *Educational Leadership*, 45, 2, pp. 64–67; Simon, A. (1977) 'Analyzing educational platforms: A supervisory strategy', *Educational Leadership*, 34, 8, pp. 580–585; Fuller, F. and Manning, B. (1973) 'Self confrontation reviewed: A conceptualization for video playback in teacher education', *Review of Educational Research*, 34, p. 487.

15 See Argyris and Schon (1974) *op. cit.*, and Argyris, C. (1982) *Reasoning, Learning and Action: Individual and Organizational*, San Francisco, Jossey-Bass.

16 See McNeil, L. (1986) *Contradictions of Control: School Structure and School Knowledge*, London, Routledge and Kegan Paul.

Chapter 8

Leadership, Vision and Dramatic Consciousness

The drama of schooling can continue on a mindless, unreflective course indefinitely. If educators in a given school are to transform the drama of schooling into an international, self-reflecting, self-correcting drama in which schooling for the drama of life takes place, then it will call for leadership on the part of all in that educational community. What does this kind of leadership involve? Fortunately the recent literature in leadership enables us to understand the general shape it may take. A brief review of that literature will illustrate how compatible recent thinking on leadership is with the notion of dramatic consciousness developed above. That thinking about leadership also enables us to link up with our metaphors of player, coach, director and critic.

Recent Literature on Leadership

Leadership research and theory has moved away from an earlier, instrumental view of leadership towards what some have labeled a more substantive view of leadership.[1] Earlier treatments of leadership, strongly influenced by behavioristic psychology and positivistic sociology, tended to reduce leadership to a few observable variables such as human relations, decision making, productivity, etc. More recently, however, the works of Gardiner,[2] Bennis and Nanus,[3] Burns,[4] and Vaill[5] have introduced into the literature on leadership terms such as vision, symbolic meaning, purpose, culture, transformation. These authors have stressed the need people have to find a larger meaning to their work than technical efficiency, a need to be part of a larger effort to make a difference in society, a need to be part of a group striving for standards of quality and excellence that will set the pace in their profession.[6]

For our purposes the term 'vision' proves especially pertinent. As we probe what the term means, where it comes from, how it gets expressed, how it binds both leaders and followers and how it becomes embodied in the institution, we will see how this analysis of leadership relates to our understanding of dramatic consciousness and to the activities of the players, coaches, directors and critics of the drama of schooling.

Vision and its Sources

Most of the authors who use the term vision, or its correlates, 'purpose' or 'mission' do not provide very specific descriptions of what it means. In its deeper sense it signifies an ideal state of affairs, the passionate commitment to which drives leaders and followers to an intense and focused striving. Others such as Andrews use it in a more concrete sense as referring to a standard to be achieved by all (such as reading at grade level by all tenth grade students, or achieving above-average test scores on other standardized tests).[7] Such a vision provides the drive and energy in schools serving at-risk children. On the other hand, it is not a large vision of the many magnificent things these children could achieve.

Where does the vision of an ideal school come from? In any given school, the vision may emerge over time, spreading out from a few key people on the staff who share and exemplify that vision with others. But where does it originate in the originators? Eisenstadt, commenting on Weber's concept of charismatic leadership, says that the way one arrives at a vision and the specific cultural expression which embodies that vision, will vary in a thousand ways.[8] But the vision has its roots in those deep, core meanings about human life, its dignity, grandeur, beauty, value, etc. It tends to be expressed in myth, poetry amd metaphor. It is concerned with values such as freedom, honor, selflessness, loyalty, devotion to community, integrity and dignity of the person, equality, peace and harmony among peoples, the rule of law, the elevation of reason and civility, wisdom, self governance, courage, character, a perfect performance, creative expression, harmony with nature, etc.

Efforts to pinpoint where one's vision came from will trail off into many strands in one's personal and professional history. Sometimes one can point to several circumstances which reinforced a particular conviction, circumstances such as the example of one's father, the moralizing of a popular teacher, a painful experience during one's first year of teaching. In other instances, the vision will take shape over many years of reading. In other instances the vision will be borrowed from one or two very influential persons in one's professional career. What is crucial in every case, however, is that those influences express fundamental beliefs about human life, about what it means to be an authentic human being, about what holds social life and communities together, about which values help us to make sense of the confusion that surrounds us. Those influences shape one's basic beliefs and ground what emerges as one's vision of education.

A vision of education, if it is to be anything more than a collection of prescribed platitudes about schools, must be grounded in those meanings basic to human life. That does not require the thinking of a professional philosopher. It does require, however, that educators reflect on what they believe to be the values and meanings basic to human life, and that they reflect on whether they practise those beliefs in their work in schools.

The Expression of Vision

Vision is expressed in a variety of ways. Some educators express their vision through scenarios of their ideal school. Such scenarios, which require some imagination, provide short vignettes that embody the core values of the vision of schooling. They might take a format such as the following. 'Let me tell you about a typical history class in my ideal school. As the class begins...' 'Let me tell you about a typical discplinary situation in my school. It begins with the teacher and the counselor...' 'Let me tell you about a typical staff development exercise in my ideal school...'

Some visions of schooling will be expressed in a formal mission statement. 'The mission of Overbottom School is threefold. First...'. Sometimes that mission statement is preceded by a philosophy statement. 'Overbottom School is guided by a philosophy that holds for the absolute inviolability of the individual, as well as the individual's absolute responsibility to contribute to the welfare of the community. Under such a philosophy, Overbottom School conceives of its mission as...'.

Other expressions of vision will take the form of a series of yearly, school-wide objectives. These yearly objectives, while never encompassing the vision entirely, begin to express the vision cumulatively as, year after year, they reveal the long-term agenda of the school. The staff of the school may have found it difficult at any one time to express the complete vision, but looking back on those yearly objectives, they can understand how their intuitions were guided by some tacit sense of the whole.

Other educators will use the cultural traditions of the school to express their vision. They can point to the school motto, the school song, the school mascot and other cultural artefacts long associated with the history of the school to highlight certain values which the school has traditionally espoused. Others will look to the culture or the cultures of the people the school has served to highlight some special or unique value in those cultures which have important implications for the fundamental character of the school. Telling stories about former students or teachers who are heroes in the eyes and memories of the people in the community also tends to promote those values central to the vision of the school.

Other educators are better engineers than rhetoricians. They will point to specific policies, structures and programs in their school as embodying the vision of the schools. To them words do not matter as much as those relatively permanent organizational arrangements that channel energy and attention toward those values and meanings that lie at the core of the school's vision.

The best expression of an educational vision, of course, would encompass all of the above varieties of expression. It would indicate that the vision of the school had indeed penetrated the entire life of the school.

Overcoming the Leader-Follower Dichotomy

A common understanding of leadership implies a dichotomy between leader and followers. The leader has vision; the followers accept the leader's vision and accommodate their actions to the leader's vision. In the case of a school, the assumption would be that the principal has a vision and coerces or cajoles the staff to accept that vision. That is to misunderstand the true nature of leadership, however. The vision must be composed, shared and owned by the majority of the community. The leader's power does not come so much from legal authority or from professional authority as much as it comes from a vision of the community itself, shared and owned by the community. Lacking a shared vision, administrators rely on legal and professional authority, but that merely leads to legal and professional compliance on the part of the staff. When a staff works together under the inspiration and motivation of a shared vision, leadership is a quality that all on the staff begin to exercise. The vision of what the community is capable of and desirous of striving for draws on and focuses the collective energy and talent of the members of the community. The principal may engage the community in defining and attending to their vision. Their vision is sometimes influenced by the principal's expression of the vision. Nevertheless, the vision expressed by the whole community has to express the community's dreams for itself.

The energy and enthusiasm of the staff and students tends, when unfocused by a community purpose, to follow individualistic, self-serving goals. These inevitably lead to tensions, arguments over scarce resources, defensive behavior, unhealthy competition, a focus on external rewards. When that energy is focused by a common vision, and a vision which calls forth the best in everyone, then that community has an enormous reservoir of power to achieve something wonderful. Leaders try to keep the community focused on the vision because the power for greatness comes not from the leader but from the communal vision of greatness.[9]

Institutionalizing the Vision

The word 'institutionalize' has two very different meanings. A common meaning signifies the act of putting someone away in a place which treats people with special problems. Most frequently it is equated with the suggestion, 'Put that fellow in the booby-hatch'. A second meaning of the word is to make a new element or program a part of an institution. Some companies, for example, wish to institutionalize a more creative way of thinking, or a new approach to human resource development. By that they mean that the company should initiate procedures for identifying, rewarding and utilizing these new elements; creative thinking, or human resource development must be embodied in the structures and processes, policies and programs of the company. An innovation that is not institutionalized remains on the periphery, the concern of a few people, perhaps, but it will have little impact on the overall life of the institution.

The literature on change and innovation offers insight into the process of institutionalization.[10] It points to a three stage process that moves from an initiation stage, to an implementation stage, to an institutionalization stage. The initiation stage involves naming the problem or issue facing the organization, getting consensus that there is a problem or issue that needs to be addressed, discussing various alternative responses to the problem and the probable consequences of each response, and choosing what seems to be the best possible response, given the limitations of resources and the goals and the needs of the organization. The implementation stage involves training of personnel in the new skills and aptitudes required by the change, allocation of administrative responsibility, establishing channels of communication and feedback, authorizing budgetary allocations, assignment of specific responsibilities to those carrying out the change, setting up bridging mechanisms to other elements in the ordinary operation of the organization, ensuring the stability and job security of people involved in the implementation. The institutionalization stage involves following through on all of the implementation efforts so that people involved have a sense of mastery of the new understandings and skills, so that the innovation affects more and more people, or it comes into use by more and more people, so that the innovation becomes integrated into the schedule of the day and week, becomes a piece of the operating budget, and is seen as strengthening the overall productivity or climate of the organization.

Hence, it is evident that having a vision is only one element of leadership. Bringing that vision into the life blood of the school requires a large, cooperative effort on the part of the whole staff. It will require a careful evaluation of the everyday life of the school, and of those policies, programs, structures and procedures which organize and govern the everyday life of the school. Frequently, the educational vision of the school will run into the confining walls of the bureaucratic organization of the school: departmentalization, grade levels, the daily class schedule, the weekly schedule, budgetary limitations, authority and responsibility conflicts. Rarely will the organization come close to the perfect embodiment of the educational vision. Having said that, there is much space for movement toward that perfect embodiment of the vision in the institution.

Vision and Dramatic Consciousness

The above analysis of leadership and the crucial importance of vision suggests an ideal view of a school that is actively and intentionally engaged in the drama of schooling, with a faculty collectively exercising leadership under the guidance of a commonly shared vision. At face value, that could appear a facile but empty generalization or a frightening desire for uniformity. The possibility, however, is more complex and flexible. Vision is never exactly the same for everyone in the school. Each teacher will express the elements of the school vision in unique and personal ways. Furthermore, the teaching of a variety of academic subjects will of necessity require a rich variety of approaches and strategies. Given the plurality of talents, interests and backgrounds of the students, the influence of the school's vision on the students will be embodied in a multiplicity of ways.

In a given school — our focus is always on the individual school, not on a local or state system — the vision of the school offers to the educating community an exciting view of possibilities. The vision of what a school could or might achieve is always out in front of them, drawing them on by the attraction of the rich human possibilities for each member of the school community. The vision is the dream, the ideal, the richest fulfilment of the possibilities inherent in the human talent and energy and spirit of each and all.

Every teacher's vision is made up of the dreams of possibilities for the students, possibilities growing out of the activity of the student on the subject matter and of the subject matter working on the student. Those dreams will not be wildly unrealistic, for teachers learn very quickly that growth usually comes in millimeters, but they will be ambitious enough to urge the student always to take the next necessary step toward their next personal best performance. For the English teacher, it may be the dream of the polished and insightful composition, or the intricately textured poem which each student is capable of writing. For the science teacher, it may be the ideal laboratory report which not only clearly expresses the measurements and conclusions of the experiment, but goes beyond to pose intriguing questions waiting further testing. For the social studies teacher, it may be that special moment of a student's insight into the balance between large social forces intersecting at a given point in history and the human choices, heroic or cowardly, which ignite the explosive power in those forces.

The vision of the possible constitutes the heart of dramatic consciousness. Awareness of the possibilities in every learning opportunity is awareness of the intrinsic drama of schooling, for every learning opportunity issues in growth or defeat — no matter how small. If the result is failure, how do the teacher and student respond to it? Their response to failure can turn it into a growth experience if they both learn something from the failure. The habit of learning from failure and defeat can be, in fact, one of the most significant life-long learnings of schooling, for most people fail more often than succeed in the trial and error drama of living.

Vision, then, leads to a heightened dramatic consciousness because vision enlarges the possibilities of the drama. When every teacher in a school brings that dramatic consciousness to his or her work with youngsters, and they share the same basic vision with the school administration, then that vision is on the way to being instituionalized in the school. The energy and insight flowing from the dramatic consciousness of teachers will lead them to improvise new learning activities, rehearse new approaches, reorganize the sets of the classroom and the time schedules of the scenes so that the dramatic possibilities of the learning situation may be more fully realized.

Some of the recent school reform literature speaks of 'teacher empowerment'.[11] That term means different things to different groups; teacher unions see it one way, administrators see it another way.[12] Without denying that teachers need a political power base to make their concerns known in the halls of local and state governments, and without denying that teachers need more control over the bureaucratic impositions on their professional autonomy, nevertheless, there is an understanding of empowerment that goes to the heart of the question.

Empowerment means having power to do something. That power can be a legal power; it can be an organizational power, it can be a power deriving from one's professional training and expertise. In the sense that we would use the term as applying to the drama of schooling, empowerment is the power one has as a human being to engage in the drama of one's own life and in the drama of one's life with others. It is not power over someone. It is not the power deriving from academic degrees or legal authority, although those are not discounted. Rather it is the power of being a human being, the power of being who you are, the power of taking yourself seriously and taking others seriously and choosing to be that way and to act that way. No legal, bureaucratic or professional power confers that power; it is ours as human beings. Sometimes that power must be exercised in resistance to legal, bureaucratic or professional power. At other times, that power will be supported by legal, bureaucratic and professional power, as the teacher-empowerment literature would have it.

Teacher empowerment in this deeper sense, then, means the power to enter into the human drama of everyday life, which for teachers takes place, to a large degree, within the drama of schooling. That power is enormously enhanced when teachers have a vision of the dramatic possibilities in the drama of schooling. That power is energized by the desire to bring to fulfilment the enormous potential in the human beings one works with. Dramatic consciousness, fueled by vision, empowers teachers and administrators to exercise leadership as directors, coaches, critics and players in the drama of schooling.

A cynic will say that this all sounds embarrassingly Pollyanna-ish. Teachers' and administrators' lives are terribly circumscribed by contextual, not to mention pathological, constraints. The contentious and litigious character of public life leaves little or no room for this kind of free, autonomous choice. To encourage this kind of phantasy drama seems reckless in the extreme. Our argument for the power to choose one's life would not deny contextual and psychological limitations to these choices. On the other hand, the greatest limitation to this kind of power is the belief that one does not possess it. Moreover, it is to the advantage to those who wish to exercise control over the social drama to have us believe that. Not to believe that one has the power to choose to engage as a free and autonomous subject in the human drama, reduces the human drama to a monstrous puppet show. It is precisely the vocation of teaching to empower youngsters against that interpretation of human life, and to empower them for the improvisation of human freedom within the ever present limitations of the context of their choices.

Notes

1 For an overview of the earlier and more recent literature on leadership, see

Sergiovanni, T. and Starratt, R. (1988) *Supervision: Human Perspectives*, 4th ed., New York, McGraw-Hill, chapters 7 and 8.

2 Gardiner, J. (1986, 1987) The *Nature of Leadership: Introductory Consideration*, Leadership Papers/1; *The Tasks of Leadership*, Leadership Papers/2; *The Heart of the Matter*, Leadership Papers/3; *Leadership and Power*, Leadership Papers/4; *The Moral Aspect of Leadership*, Leadership Papers/5, Washington, DC, The Independent Sector.

3 Bennis, W. and Nanus, B. (1985) *Leaders: The Strategies of Taking Charge*, New York, Harper and Row.

4 Burns, J. (1978) *Leadership*, New York, Harper Torchbooks.

5 Vaill, P. (1989) *Managing as a Performing Art*, San Francisco, Jossey-Bass.

6 See Sergiovanni and Starratt (1988) *op. cit.*, pp. 201–213, for an attempt to mold the ideas of the above authors into an integrated theory of leadership.

7 Brandt, R. (1987) 'On leadership and student achievement: A conversation with Richard Andrews', *Educational Leadership*, 45, 1, pp. 9–16.

8 Eisenstadt, S. (1968) *Max Weber: On Charisma and Institution Building*, Chicago, University of Chicago Press.

9 See Burns, J. (1978) *op. cit.*, chapters 16 and 17, for an incisive treatment of transformational leadership.

10 See Miles, M. (1983) 'Unraveling the mystery of institutionalization', *Educational Leadership*, 41, 3, pp. 14–19; Zaltman, G., Duncan, R. and Holbeck, J. (1973) *Innovations and Organizations*, New York, John Wiley.

11 Maeroff, G. (1988) *The Empowerment of Teachers*, New York, Teachers College Press; The Holmes Group (1986) *Tomorrow's Teachers*, Lansing, MI.

12 Iorio, J. (1988, Summer) 'Empowerment and governance, a revolutionary and evolutionary process', *Journal of School Administrators' Association of New York State*.

Chapter 9

Players, Coaches, Directors, Critics

We are close to rounding out our understanding of the drama of schooling as the schooling of drama. The drama of schooling involves scripts within scripts within scripts: academic scripts, bureaucratic scripts, personal scripts, social scripts; within those scripts there are ideological, aesthetic, cosmological, ethical and epistemological scripts. Often those scripts are confused with each other, or are substituted one for the other.

Schooling is about forming individual characters as well as forming a people, within which and from which community individual characters derive social significance in the drama. Teaching and administering in the drama of schooling requires awareness of the large and the small dramas being rehearsed aned enacted. Leadership in the drama of schooling requires a grasp of the essential meanings of the drama, a vision of how the drama might unfold. Dramatic consciousness of students, teachers and administrators, sensitivity to the nature of the drama they are all enagaged in, enables them to participate and construct the drama more intentionally. We turn to that activity now, the action of the players, coaches, directors and critics.

One of the major tragedies of the drama of life is that a person might miss his or her own life, in the same way one misses a plane.[1] Often that missing of life results from a fear of choosing one's destiny or a fear of humiliation and ridicule if one freely expresses one's longings for full living. There is a sense of utter aloneness in the choice to be oneself, as indeed is fitting, for no-one else can tell another who to be. In choosing to follow one's own compass, one orphans oneself. Previously parents and those in authority provided direction, advice and sometimes coercion in the journey of becoming an authentic person. There is safety and security in letting others assume responsibility for one's life. Once one steps out from the group and declares one's freedom, that safety and security are lost. There is a feeling of being alone, over and against the world and all the possible disasters that can fall from the sky. Some people, afraid of the beast crouching with menacing mien in the underbrush, remain in a state of relative dependency all of their lives, waiting for the next turn in the road to point to unambiguously predictable horizons.

Such fears can also lead to a neurotic compulsion to control one's environment entirely.[2] Because one cannot tolerate unpredictability in oneself or in others, because allowing people to be free and spontaneous could only unmask one's fragile sense of self worth, then the threat of living must be reduced to a manageable scale. The script must be fixed for everyone; then there is no risk, no chance for a slip-up which would expose one's nakedness.

Schools are places where children and youth can learn how to make autonomous choices, how to become a character in their own right, not simply a costumed mannequin positioned as part of the scenery in someone else's drama. To reduce the fear, and to tailor the task to the capabilities of the youngsters, those choices are necessarily small choices. Sometimes they are inappropriate choices. The strength of trial and error learning, however, is that one can learn from errors, as well as successes.

Schools also teach children and youth about the world in which one becomes an individual. There is a natural world which works in such and such ways. There are ways to use this natural world which respect the rhythms and harmonies in nature, and there are other ways which destroy them. There are also dangers to be avoided in the natural world, dangers such as swimming in icy waters, or walking through poison ivy, or picking up snakes. There is a social world, with its customs and traditions, its various races and nationalities and cultures, its history of heroic achievement and repulsive atrocities. There are responsibilities which individuals have to their communities, and there are a variety of outlets for individual expression within the cultural patterns of those communities. This world also involves the world of work wherein one expresses talents and interests, wherein one makes a contribuiton to the community, wherein one earns a livelihood to meet a variety of survival and recreational needs. There is a personal and interpersonal world revealed in the humantities and the arts, as well as in the human sciences. This world is a world wherein one becomes a somebody, a unique and priceless being who sings a unique song, writes a unique story, makes a unique contribution to the world, becomes a hero as no other person on the face of the earth can.

In other words, schools help youngsters weave the fabric of intelligibility with which they clothe their immediate world. That fabric of intelligibility enables them to clothe themselves, to choose who and how they will be, to become a persona, to put on the external mask and costume, to write the lines that express themselves. That fabric of intelligibility enables them to interpret the words and gestures of others in their environment, to understand what others mean when they express themselves through their masks and costumes and script. It enables them to join in with others in the drama of living, both inside and outside the school.

Actors

The most obvious actors in the drama of schooling are the students. They are the primary ones for whom the drama is structured. They are the ones who fail or succeed in the drama of schooling. They are the ones for whom the rehearsals of learning are conducted. They are the actors expected to learn the academic script, as well as the bureaucratic script.

Students become actors in the drama of schooling by learning the scripts which the coaches and directors put before them. They not only memorize the script, but they so absorb the script that it enables them to express themselves through the script. This applies not only to the script of language and vocabulary, number and formula, but also to the substance of the academic script, whether that involves the meanings in geography, life science, literature, or civics. In other words, the script opens up a world for them, a world they enter and inhabit. When they talk about that world, they talk about it in terms of what it means to them, in terms of their life and how they understand themselves in relation to that world. An oriental child of a recently arrived immigrant family will absorb the script differently than a child whose forebears were present at the founding of the nation. A black child will relate school learnings to a cultural heritage in the home that differs from that in a white home. A hearing-impaired child will relate to school learnings differently than a sight-impaired child.

This personalization of learning does not negate the common expression of that learning which tests demand and certain uniformities of daily life require. Water can be expressed as H_2O on a test, but the word can also carry memories of a favourite waterfall, a cool drink, the sound of waves breaking on the rocks. The memorized dates of the 'discovery' of America or of Australia are used to pass common exams. What the discovery means to the American Indian child, or the Australian Aboriginal child, however, will differ from the meaning to the descendant of one of the original European settlers of those countries. Those historical events fit into radically different scripts about the formation of those peoples and about their present day identities. Tests rarely touch upon those historical meanings.

Nevertheless, there are relatively well established bodies of knowledge in the sciences which are proposed as making up a fixed academic script. To be sure, there are enormous bodies of information about the natural and human world which need to be absorbed and understood. However, these bodies of knowledge are often presented as though they were to be mastered for their own sake, with little or no reference to their significance for human living. Although it may not be possible in every instance to draw some relationship to human living from a given piece of the academic script, whenever it is possible, it should be attempted. We tend to learn with greater understanding those things that are related to our life. That kind of learning is intrinsically more useful in the service of human living.

Learning how to Act with a Problematic Script

In relatively stable historical periods, schooling involves a relatively stable script. There would be room for improvisation on an individual level, but the standard cues, customs, traditions, conceptual frameworks, patterns of gesture and speech would be available for the improviser's creative use as well as serve as a channel for that creative use.

In times of rapid change and fluid social movements, however, the script is not as fixed, and improvisation moves more and more toward a continuously makeshift extemporaneity. Certainly this is true for younger women who must find their way, sometimes quite painfully, without familiar sex role sign posts, or even with an appropriate language to discuss with one another their experience. Similarly, the shift to an information based economy, has brought new understandings of power, of work, of knowledge itself, whose implications for the conduct of the social drama are not fully scripted.

In today's drama of schooling there will necessarily be a blend of tradition and novelty, as the social drama calls for new relationships between the sexes, between racial and ethnic communities, between social classes, between political and economic entities on both the national and international levels. Some traditions cannot be retained in their present form; they require reinterpretation so that the underlying human purposes they served can be appreciated, even while the forms that clothed traditions may change. Hence, in today's school, students have to be involved in learning for the drama in explicitly active and constructive ways. They have to be challenged to look at the fluid social drama with all its possibilities and challenges, and to invent potential scripts by which the drama can be carried forward to serve basic human purposes. To do this, of course, they will need a foundation of basic information, the basic tools of language, logic, negotiating and exploratory skills, information processing and application skills, and a sense of human values which grounds the social drama. Those understandings, skills and values, however, must be taught, not in some abstract, isolated social vacuum, but precisely as tools for the carrying forward of the social drama. Schooling for one's exclusively private, personal advancement is ultimately self defeating, for it denies the social nature of the drama of life.

Actors learn the script and do something with it. They manipulate numbers, measure weights and movement, play a musical instrument, shape a pot, argue a political cause, analyze a poem, compose a map, explain the principles of magnetic energy. They either rehearse acting upon the world with their knowledge, or they improvise such action directly. They engage others in this action on the world by cooperating on a project. Sometimes they influence other persons directly through persuasion to take action on the world, as in political referenda.

In other words, the actor is a source of action, a source of choices, a subject which initiates action and engages the world, a presence to be reckoned with, a force in the scene, someone who fabricates something or makes something happen. Actors are essential to the drama. Without actors there is no drama. In the drama of schooling, were all the actors to act in totally uniform, predictable ways, there would be no drama. For the drama to be authentically human the actors require some latitude to make the script their own, and to use the script to express themselves. As they attempt to use the script to express themselves, they will make mistakes and misunderstand some parts of the script. That is why schooling involves rehearsal time, so that actors can find how the script works, which is to say, how the world works and how it might work.

Teachers as Actors

Teachers are also actors in the drama of schooling. Their acting, however, implies a triangular relationship with the student and the subject under consideration. Understanding the script, and a variety of ways the script may be expressed, as well as understanding the individual students who make up the class with their interests, talents, limitations and family backgrounds, teachers rehearse the academic script with students in such a variety of ways that the script comes alive for them. Sometimes the personalities of teachers and students become clashing forces in the drama, as when a teacher tries to control an unruly student, or a group of students attempt to make a teachers' life miserable on any given day. Sometimes the teacher must heighten the drama of learning by teasing students or coaxing them to take a longer look, or by nudging the material under their noses. Sometimes the teacher must engage the personal drama of the student, as when a youngster is having a major battle with a parent, or is depressed over the loss of a friend. This form of the drama usually takes place off the set of the classroom and involves not so much the academic script as it does the larger script of interpersonal living.

Teachers are actors at other levels of the drama of schooling. There are many behind-the-scene meetings, planning sessions, committee projects which involve the action of teachers. At this level, the teachers work together to monitor the school drama, to coordinate the rehearsals of the day or week, to plan for improvements in the script or to work through a new version of the plot.

In the above instances, teachers are actors by performing the roles of coach, director and critic. As directors, teachers keep reminding students and themselves of the basic plot in the drama of schooling, namely, that they are involved in learning how to conduct the drama of living. As coaches they rehearse the understanding of the tapestry of meaning embedded in the script, or they explore with their students ways to unearth or create meanings in the imperfectly scripted scenes in the larger social drama. As critics, they monitor the performance of the school drama, calling attention to flawed performances, not only of the students, but of themselves. As critics, they ask the difficult questions. As critics, they also remind the company of the basic plot behind the drama.

Administrators as Actors

Administrators play active roles in the drama of schooling by similar involvement as coach, director and critic. Although not directly involved, for the most part, in coaching students, administrators sometimes coach the coaches through involvement in classroom supervision and staff development programs. Sometimes administrators simply arrange and support coaching clinics whereby teachers learn the art of coaching from each other and perhaps a recognized master coach. However administrators' involvement with coaches is realized, their part in the drama must clearly include a commitment to caring for the coaches and for the quality of their coaching.

As directors of the drama of schooling, principals can influence the drama in a variety of ways. As a leader who articulates the vision of the drama of schooling as the schooling of drama, the principal facilitates the intentional focus on the dramatic elements within the school. The principal is the one who often reminds the coaches and the players what the drama is for. Using metaphors describing the social drama and its challenges, the principal can constantly clothe even mundane classes on basic learnings with dramatic significance. Furthermore, the principal can suggest ways of reorganizing the use of space and time, money and curriculum resources so that the drama of schooling is enhanced.

As critic the principal exercises additional influence on the drama of schooling. Here the emphasis would not be so much on criticizing individual, poor performances on the part of students and teachers, but rather in insisting that teachers and students assess their own performance, that they constantly reflect on the quality of the school drama, that they review the standards of quality to which they hold themselves accountable, that they remind themselves continually that the purpose of the schooling of drama is to serve basic human aspirations. In this capacity, the principal may invite others skilled in the art of criticism to visit the school and to train teachers and students in criticism of the drama.

If a society wishes to be self renewing, then, as John Gardiner suggests, it must be skilled in self criticism.[3] Its citizens must be 'loving critics', however, not destructive or cynical critics. Without this spirit and skill in criticism, the drama can all too often become self serving, its script no longer allowing improvisation, the plot no longer open to new possibilities. The principal is one of the chief guardians of the integrity of the drama of schooling, and hence the role of critic is essential.

Involvement in the Drama of Living

Principals and teachers, like their students, are themselves involved in the drama of living. In their personal lives they face the everyday joys and challenges of living. Their involvement in the drama of schooling does not exhaust their roles. They are spouse, parent, son or daughter, friend or relative, voter, consumer, neighbor, hiker, volunteer, church member and a host of other things. As unique human beings, they have their song to sing, their story to write, their ways of being heroes. When they play their roles in the drama of schooling, they bring their unique personalities, talents, interests, biases and needs to the roles. In so doing, they model for their youngsters in school ways of being human, ways of engaging in the drama of living. They also bring their personal experience to the task of educating, experience which acts as both lens and filter to their performance as educators.

In their involvement in the drama of schooling, they, too, need to pause and reflect on how they see and understand the larger human drama. They need to take the time to enrich their own participation in that larger drama. They need to discuss how their work relates to that drama. In other words, they have to be actors, players, present to each other as full human beings, not simply as employees of the school system, roll players in the smaller drama of school life. Unless they grow to accept each other as legitimate and integral players in the larger drama, they cannot learn from one another the many lessons in wisdom that the drama of life itself teaches, lessons which ought to enter into the script of schooling. Furthermore, unless they share in a trusting exchange, accepting each other's differences and talents, then their participation in the schooling of drama will be seen as unauthentic, for they will be seen, not as a community, but as isolated, disconnected individuals who do not model what they are trying to teach. Hence participation in the schooling of drama implies genuine participation in that drama of life. In turn, participation in that drama of life enriches one's involvement in the drama of schooling.

Notes

1 See Walker Percy's brilliant novel, (1980) *The Second Coming*, New York, Farrar, Straus and Giroux, p. 123. Ernest Becker makes the same point in his critique of Freudian psychology. See Becker, E. (1973) *The Denial of Death*, New York, The Free Press.
2 See Becker, E. (1975) *Escape From Evil*, New York, The Free Press.
3 Gardiner, J. (1963) *Self Renewal*, New York, Harper and Row.

Chapter 10

Grounding the Analogy in Classroom Observation

Analyzing schooling by means of the analogy of drama remains an exercise in speculation or philosophy unless it is empirically grounded in at least some of the activity that takes place in schools. Can one actually see students rehearsing, teachers coaching, principals directing, people following various scripts? What does improvisation actually look like in a school setting? What are some examples of ways schools form character? Do we ever see teachers coaching youngsters in the drama of living?

One doctoral dissertation is being completed and several others are to be mounted which will provide a broadly based empirical testing of the analogy. Meanwhile, some initial observations of a handful of classrooms were conducted, charting the activities observed by means of categories developed in the preceding chapters. Questions such as the following guided the observations: What is the script being learned? (Academic scripts; bureaucratic scripts; life scripts.) Is what is happening a drama? Is it a drama of schooling only, or is it also a schooling of the drama of living? Can various activities of the teachers be described as directing, coaching, critiquing? Is there any indication of reflective practice? Are students genuine players in the drama? Does their being players seem to affect the depth of learning involved?

What follows are brief accounts of six classrooms and a commentary on how they exemplified some or all of the analogy. Details have been altered to prevent the identification of students and teachers.

Classroom Episode #1

This is a ninth grade English class in a private boarding school. The teacher, a recent graduate from a liberal arts college, has been working his way through the story, *Flowers for Algernon*. In this class, he does some dramatic reading of the story and intermittently asks members of the class to read. From time to time he breaks into the reading to point out something in the text and to ask a few questions. The teacher seems intent on coaching the class how to read a story for clues to the development of the main character, and how to detect irony in the double meanings within the text. He calls their attention to specific words and phrases and questions them to see whether they are getting the point the author is suggesting. The students who are asked to read do so in a halting, droning voice, with no apparent feeling for the character. The class concludes with a homework assignment to read the next ten pages of the story.

Commentary

It is not clear how he is using the book. The underlying script being taught seems to be the academic script, namely, 'This is how you figure out the meaning of a piece of literature'. The teacher was the performer; the students the audience, for the most part. The teacher appeared to be focused on single loop learning, namely, how to appreciate the subtle clues the author gives to following the development of the character. He never poses the questions, 'Why are we reading this story? What does Charley have to teach us?' The drama of schooling, at least in this class, seemed to have little reference to the drama of the students' lives. The teacher communicated empathy for Charley in the tone of voice he used when he was reading Charley's words, but he never asked his students, 'How would you feel if you were Charley? 'He never raised issues about how handicapped people are treated in society, although I suspect his very choice of the story was to develop at least implicit empathy for them.

There was no explicit formation of character in the class. Although the text offered many opportunities for identification with the character, the teacher never paused to ask, 'Did you ever feel like that?' or 'Isn't there a little bit of Charley in all of us?' Neither was there any effort to form a people who would accept handicapped persons as authentic members of the community. He did, however, raise the question whether Charley was unfairly stereotyped by his fellow workers as dumb. The general tenor of the class, however, seemed to indicate that there was very little of the schooling of the social drama going on, except through the influence of the story itself.

Classroom Episode #2

This is a tenth grade geometry class in a predominantly white, working-class high school. The boys all sat on one side of the room, the girls on the other. The boys wore various kinds of distinctive clothing, many with the names of hard rock musical groups stencilled on their shirts. Many girls tended to sit almost zombie-like in their seats, rarely volunteering an answer. The boys were constantly fidgeting, fooling around with the fellow next to them whenever the teacher wasn't looking.

The teacher began the class with several worksheets containing various types of figures. The class was asked to identify the figures according to the labels they had learned in earlier classes, labels such as 'triangle, rectangle, pentagon', etc. Each student worked silently on the worksheets while the teacher walked up and down the aisles commenting, praising, correcting. The teacher allowed considerable time for the completion of this work. By the time she was ready to move on, the room was very noisy, with the boys, especially, comparing notes, throwing papers and generally fooling around. Yet when the teacher stood at the front of the room and stared at them silently, the noise died down and she continued. She put a diagram of a triangle and a rectangle on the board and asked the class to comment on the differences between the interior angles of both figures. This drew some intelligent responses from a boy with a rock band emblem on the back of his shirt. Immediately after giving his answer, however, two boys near him began mocking him for cooperating with the teacher.

The teacher never verbally corrected any classroom misbehavior. Her silence brought the class to silence. Her non-reinforcement of inappropriate behavior by apparent disregard led to the cessation of that behavior. For the most part, she kept the class on task through a carefully prepared set of activities. It was apparent, however, that for many of the boys attention was grudgingly given; during the few moments of transition between the teacher's prepared activities, those boys reverted to the more important activity of fooling around with their peers. It was difficult to know what was going on with the girls; they seemed to stay very much inside themselves.

Commentary

There were two dramas going on during the class: one was the drama of schooling, with the teacher trying to get students to attend to the academic script (learning the language of geometry and understanding how the world of geometry works); the other drama was the drama of early teenage boys seeking self esteem by resisting the adult world of school and carrying on their games of showing each other how funny, witty, cynical, or macho they could be. The teacher, while being aware of the second drama, made no concessions to it, never drawing out possible relationships between the drama of geometry and the drama of design problems with cars or jewelry, or the geometry of a soccer match. The teacher and the students had agreed to tolerate each other's dramas, as long as they didn't seriously impinge on one another.

There was no schooling of the drama of living and hence the drama of schooling received the students' minimum attention necessary to comply with the minimum learning of the academic script. Oddly enough, there was formation of character going on, but it was under the students' direction; it was the formation of resistance either by expressive behaviors, or by withdrawal. Certainly the separation of the sexes by seating arrangements, whether chosen by the teacher or by the students, was not conducive to cooperative activities between the boys and girls; there was little evidence of any effort to form a people in that class.

Classroom Episode #3

This episode takes place in a parochial, inner-city elementary school serving mostly Hispanic and Black students. The teacher, a white haired Hispanic nun, had been discussing a story with her fifth grade class for the past two days and was now drawing out some implications of the story. The story involved a woman winning a speedboat race in competition with a group of men. The teacher referred to the status of women and their ability to compete in a 'man's world'. She gave her view on the lack of opportunities for women to compete on an equal basis with men. She cited examples of superior female achievement: Margaret Thatcher of Britain, Golda Meir of Israel, Mother Theresa of Calcutta. She spoke of the many women now moving into previously male dominated fields such as medicine, law, engineering, business, the space program. She then invited students to comment and give opinions.

The boys responded first, giving examples of things women could not do: women were not as strong as men; they could not run as fast; they were not as smart as men; they could not earn as much money as men. The students became more and more animated, with the girls booing and hissing the comments of the boys and the boys applauding a telling comment by one of their peers. The teacher promoted this exchange by frequent comments which drew additional opinions from the students. There was much laughing, interrupting and emphatic feelings generated as each group vied with each other to prove how either men or women are superior. The teacher set the tone by her own enthusiastic response to each offering, with laughter and obvious enjoyment of the debate.

The boys were then invited by the teacher to divide into teams of three to put their arguments in writing, and to cite evidence to support their position; the girls were given a similar assignment. A few minutes of noisy moving of desks into clusters of three was followed by animated discussion among the teams of three. The teacher walked around the room answering questions, making suggestions, challenging pieces of evidence being offered. After about ten minutes of this, the teacher brought the unit to a close by telling them that they would have a debate on the following day, and that each team should finish up their written statements the next morning. They would follow this up by making felt banners which illustrated the outstanding qualities of both men and women.

Commentary

This episode illustrates several elements of the analogy with drama. Clearly, the drama of schooling was heightened by the schooling of the drama of living. The teacher as director of the drama, arranged the scene so as to set up the confrontation between gender stereotyping. Once the scene was established, the teacher entered into the confrontation as a player, voicing her own opinions and encouraging the students to engage in the drama. She also acted as a coach during the discussion by asking students to clarify what they meant or by challenging them to give evidence. During the writing session she continued coaching as she moved from team to team, pointing out mistakes and asking leading questions which led the students to explore additional evidence.

The students were clearly players in the drama. They were asked to relate their views, improvising their own script within the larger script of gender stereotyping they had heard at home and on the streets. They teamed up with their peers during the discussion in a contest with the others. Yet, the laughter and the exaggerated expressions of booing and hissing let everyone know that they were playing a game, and were mocking themselves, so to speak, as each side postured for position.

The teacher as director played an important part in the schooling of drama by insisting that each side come up with evidence to support their position. In other words, the social debate about women's rights and women's grievances and men's superiority needs to be supported by some kind of objective, factual evidence; otherwise, the arguments can be shown to be merely prejudicial and ideological.

There was clearly some formation of character going on as both boys and girls were exploring what it means to be a man or a woman, as well as the kind of public role each will play. They were learning to modify opinions in the light of arguments from others and in the face of evidence to the contrary. They were learning to collaborate with others on a team project. As a class they were confronting a major cause of disunity and injustice in the contemporary social drama. This debate has implications on how they will be as people, how they will respect differences and find complementarities in differences, how they will find the community enriched by both male and female. The promised activity of making banners to display the strengths of both sexes indicates a moving away from the accent on conflict to an accent on mutual respect.

Classroom Episode #4

This is an advanced placement Spanish class in an affluent suburban high school. It is the first month of school. The teacher is reviewing basic structural aspects of the language by having the students prepare dialogues which illustrate some verb forms and tenses and moods which have been previously assigned. The teacher begins the class by reminding the students of the focus of the dialogue exercise, namely, the review of verb tenses and moods. Then he invites the first team of two students to come to the front of the room to present their dialogue.

In the first dialogue, two boys have prepared a script describing two brothers who have gone to the bakery to buy a birthday cake for their father. The dialogue contains some funny discussion about what kinds of decorations they should put on the top of the cake. Both boys are fairly animated as they play out the scene, even though they are reading the script, which they had written out together for their homework. The teacher responds with considerable praise of the performance, his comments given in Spanish. He then invites the class to ask questions of the two performers. Both questions and responses are given in Spanish, with one boy evoking laughter with his exaggerated facial gestures and theatrical speaking of the language.

The next dyad, a boy and a girl, present a story of two friends meeting at the bus stop to go to the zoo. The boy is fairly expressive in his presentation, but the girl stands very stiffly, with her head down, simply reading the Spanish script in a monotone. At the end of their dialogue, the teacher offers praise again, calling attention to two verbs which have unusual past tense forms. Again the class is invited to ask questions. A girl in the audience asks the girl in the dialogue whether the boy going to the zoo with her is her boyfriend. The girl blushes and says no, they are just friends who live on the same street. The class laughs and makes disbelieving comments. When the two students return to their seats, the girl's body returns to a more natural carriage, as though freed from a constricting mold. She laughs easily over a whispered comment from a classmate; the ordeal of being the object of everyone's attention is over.

The next dialogue, between two girls, concerns their getting a summer job. One has a job in a department store, the other has not found anything yet and is very discouraged. The first girl tries to encourage her to keep looking. They act out their parts very well, as though they had rehearsed even the gestures. At the end, the teacher exclaims, 'Bravo! Great performance!' The class applauds. The two girls beam.

After all the dialogues have been presented (there were five in all, since there were ten students in the class), the teacher goes to the front of the room and writes a page number on the board and tells them to open their books to that page for a drill exercise on some new verbs. The teacher, quite didactic now, runs through the tenses of the first few verbs and then asks various students to finish the list of verbs. Then they move quickly to a new section of the text, for translation of short paragraphs that use the verbs they have just reviewed.

The teacher is very gentle and encouraging, his tone of voice very respectful and caring of each student. He encourages them to rephrase the literal translation into a more familiar way of saying the same thing. At the end of class, before the homework assignment, the teacher refers to a mistake he made with a verb in a previous class. The class laughs gently. He uses that mistake to underscore the form of the past perfect of the verbs they have been studying.

Commentary

In this class, the teacher employs an explicit dramatic format to carry on the drama of schooling. The students have written the script, although their script has to conform to the demands of the academic script of correct verb forms. They are the script writers, the players and the directors in the dialogue exercise. The level of involvement is very obvious. One can sense it in their voices and on their faces. This is their show. They are the stars.

The drama of schooling, however, is also related to the drama of living. The ingredients of their dialogues were taken from everyday life and reflected the humor and the struggles of ordinary human beings. Moreover, each student had to go through the ordeal of being on center stage, his or her performance open to the criticism of peers as well as the teacher's. For some it was a distinct pleasure; for others, an ordeal, especially for the girl in the scene with the boy going to the zoo. Yet, that too is part of the schooling of the drama of living. One has to accept responsibility for being center stage at important times in life: job interviews, establishing life-long relationships, taking a stand on a matter of principle.

While they were working within the academic script, there was ample room for improvisation, for the expression of their unique personalities. In creating the characters in the dialogues as well as when they were paraphrasing the literal translations later in the class, the students were putting their unique stamp on the learning activity. They were in the process of creating character; the learning activity was encouraging them to be themselves. Furthermore, because they were all involved in being both actor and critic, they were learning how to accept unique expressions of individuality within a common project; without going explicitly into a reflection on it, they were experiencing themselves as a people, enjoying the contribution each one made to the class.

While the teacher let the students run the show, so to speak, for most of the class, he came back in as director and coach on the work with the textbook exercises. What was very noticeable, however, was his obvious care and gentle respect for his students. His tone of voice carried layers of positive effect. There was a lot of himself as a person in the way he dealt with the youngsters. His modeling of respect and caring seemed to be reflected in the way the audience responded to the players in the dialogues. That clearly was part of the forming of character and the forming of a people.

Classroom Episode #5

This episode involves an eleventh grade class in chemistry. The observer remembered very little from previous chemistry courses in his education, so the technical knowledge that was communicated was not grasped very well.

The teacher was conducting a demonstration lab in order to teach some general principles about chemical compounds: which ones blend easily, which ones require heat to blend, which ones remain separate even though poured into the same container (or so it seemed to the observer).

The teacher announces that he is going to do a demonstration lab. He quickly reviews some of the properties of the chemicals involved in the demonstration. He poses questions in a rapid-fire manner, seeking memorized definitions which were covered in earlier classes. He admonishes the students to raise their hands when they want to ask or answer a question (an admonition repeated about five times throughout the class period). He then passes out two sheets which contain directions about how to conduct the various experiments he will demonstrate. With that done, he moves behind the large laboratory table at the front of the room and holds up various beakers and vials of chemicals, explaining what they contain and which ones he is going to mix with which. He exhorts them to watch carefully as he demonstrates the experiment. He calls upon one of the students to read the first set of directions. He then repeats the direction as he performs the action called for by the direction: 'Alright, now I am going to check out this beaker to see that it is clean and does not contain the residue of any chemicals in an earlier experiment. What do I do next, John?' (He pauses while the student reads the direction). 'Okay, now I am going to pour in this chemical'. (He pours in a chemical from a vial). 'And now I am going to pour in this other chemical'. 'Mary, what do I do now?'

The demonstration proceeds in this fashion. At one point the teacher picks up the wrong chemical, and the student reading the directions calls out, 'No! Not that one'. The teacher had obviously chosen to make the mistake, for he follows up with, 'Why would I not want to mix that chemical with this one?' He then mocks his stupidity while the class laughs. Throughout the demonstration, he keeps asking the class rapid-fire questions: 'What is happening now?' 'What do you see?' 'Do you see a change?' 'How would you describe the reaction?' By and large the students are following him, although frequently, after two or three incorrect answers, he provides the answer.

When he has all the beakers with their compounds lined up on the table, he asks them to compare the various reactions of the chemicals when they are mixed with other chemicals. Then he says, 'Alright, let's see if we can bring this all together. Let's see what we know now from observing this experiment'. He then solicits answers from the students, and writes their observations on the board. He frequently prompts an answer, with his questions such as, 'When you look at what happened with this compound, and compare it with what happened to that compound, what do you come up with?' He labels the students responses *OBSERVATIONS*. He then writes a new category on the board, *CONCLUSIONS*. He goes on to say, 'Now we are going to ask what generalizations we may be able to make in the light of our observations, and what questions arise that need further testing'. The students seem to need a lot more coaxing and prompting to come up with statements the teacher will accept. He reminds them that they are basically following the format of a lab report. When, with some labor, they have put up on the board three conclusions and two questions, the teacher then turns to the homework assignment just before the class period ends.

Commentary

The teacher created a scene in the drama of schooling. He set the scene by asking them basic recall questions about the chemicals involved in the experiment. He announced that it would be a demonstration lab and that he would be the main performer. The students were to be the audience. With that as the basic framework, the teacher then created some interesting variations. He allowed the students to be the director of his performance. They read the directions to him and he followed them. They corrected him when he was going to mix the wrong chemical. He did what they told him to do. By being directors, the students participated in his performance at a deeper level of attention than they might have simply as a passive audience.

While being a performer, the teacher also stepped out of his role and became a director. He directed the flow of the class activities, reminding the students of the rule about raising their hands to answer a question. As director, he kept reminding the students of the point of the whole scene, namely to understand how the various properties of chemicals react differently with properties of other chemicals. At other times he specifically reminded them that they were learning the language of chemistry and the scientific method of laboratory observation. After an intervention as director, he moved back into his role as performer.

He also engaged in considerable coaching. He coached them in the skills of scientific observation and inductive reasoning. He reminded them of the properties of the chemicals, which they already knew, as they were trying to explain their observations. He also coached them in translating observations first voiced in everyday language into the language of chemistry. He would frequently ask, 'How would a chemist say that?' He also coached them in the writing of lab reports, by frequently asking, 'If you were writing that in your lab report, would it be adequate?'

Toward the end of the class, he moved out of the performer role and became a director-coach, requiring them now to perform as scientific observers of the experiment. During this time he also served as a critic, commenting on the unacceptability of certain statements for the more formal lab report format. The review of their observations brought the students to reflect on what they saw, to draw upon what they already knew and to write up a script of clear statements and conclusions. That script gradually, under the coaching and critiquing of the teacher, came to coincide with the script of the textbook and with the script expected in their lab reports — thus confirming and solidifying their grasp of how the world of chemistry works.

Was there much schooling in the drama of living in this class? There was probably some carryover into using their powers of observation and inductive reasoning in other circumstances, although the teacher made no explicit reference to that. There was no reference to the larger social drama in which chemistry plays an important part. The focus of the drama was entirely on mastering the academic script through a rehearsal of a laboratory experiment.

Classroom Episode #6

This episode takes place with a sixth grade class in an affluent suburban system. The school has encouraged homeroom teachers to conduct occasional class meetings when there was a need to discuss problems among the children. The general idea is to promote a greater sense of personal responsibility among the students so that they would all contribute to an enhanced community feeling among them. Teachers had received some brief in-service preparation for this kind of class meeting.

At the beginning of the meeting, the teacher reminds the students of the ground rules: 1. Everyone must raise their hand to be recognized to speak; 2. Everyone must respect the opinions and remarks of others, even if they do not agree with them; 3. Topics for dicussion include problems students are having with one another, problems with the staff at the school, projects the students wish to undertake. The meeting cannot be used to attack another person or to put that person on the spot.

Students and teacher were seated in a large circle. The teacher, a young, cheery woman in her third year of teaching, announced that she was calling the meeting because of reports about problems on the playground. Complaints had come in that this class was causing difficulties during the lunch recess. She asked the class to tell her the problem in their own words, reminding them that accusations of specific children would be out of place.

One girl raised her hand and said that when the sixth graders went out to the playground after lunch, sixth grade boys and fifth grade boys would start arguing over who would use the soccer playing area. The playgound supervisors were consulted but the arguments seemed to go on just about every day, leading to fights. One of the boys continued the story and said that the fifth grade boys always left lunch early and got their soccer game started before the sixth grade boys got there. They refused to let the sixth graders play in their game, or to have the grades take turns. The fights started because it wasn't fair for the fifth graders to hog the field all the time.

The teacher listened sympathetically as two other students filled in more details. She suggested that the class try to come up with a solution to the problem. One boy said that making a weekly schedule of who was to use the soccer field each day would solve the problem. One girl said that she really didn't care because the boys never let the girls play, anyway. One student suggested that they schedule lunch at different times, so that each class would have a chance to use the field.

After several additional solutions were offered, the teacher suggested that they look at how to deffuse the situation at the moment it arose. She said that the class could make up a scenario right then, with certain students volunteering to play various roles. The rest of the students would be the audience; they would make suggestions after the scene had been played.

The scenario was set up by taking comments from the previous discussion and putting them on the board:

A group of four sixth grade boys go to the soccer field. A group of four boys from the fifth grade are already there. The sixth grade boys yell, 'Get off the field, it is our turn today'. The fifth grade boys retort, 'We were here first'. One of the sixth grade boys goes to tell the supervisor. The supervisor says she really doesn't remember whose turn it is; why can't they all play together? The boys start a scuffle as one of them tries to grab the soccer ball. The supervisor then sends for the principal. All the boys are called into the principal's office and no-one gets to play.

The teacher chooses boys to play the roles; some boys resist being chosen to play the fifth grade boys. Several girls volunteer to play the part of the playgound supervisor and the principal. The scene is enacted with great realism. The audience calls out encouragement to both sides. When the boys are marched off to the principal's office, the audeience cheers wildly.

The teacher breaks the action and everyone goes back to their seats amidst much laughter and barbs tossed back and forth. The girls giggle and tease the girls who played the principal for being so 'bossy'. The teacher asks the audience for recommendations. The first few comments praised the sixth grade boys for standing up for their class. The teacher interjects, 'Remember what your task is. You are supposed to make suggestions about how the situations might have been handled better'. One of the boys suggests that they might have teams from each class which would play one another. Others comment that would simply lead to more fights. Finally one of the girls says, 'Why not have one fifth grade boy and one sixth grade boy get together with one fourth grade boy (since they occasionally use the soccer area as well) and the three of them would be in charge of working out a schedule which would allow each of the grades to use the soccer area on rotating days? We would also appoint a playground patrol made up of one boy from each of those classes who would break up fights and turn over the trouble-makers to the playgound supervisor'.

The teacher responds enthusiastically to the idea. The students voice their support. The teacher then asks who should be the boy who works on the schedule and who should be on the patrol. Almost unanimously the class points to the biggest boy in the class as the one for the playgound patrol. He scowls at this suggestion, but the teacher prevails on him to accept the appointment. They then suggest another boy, apparently the best soccer player in the class, to arrange the schedule. The teacher indicates that she will talk with the principal and the other teachers about this arrangement, and they will meet as soon as she gets the necessary approvals. The class meeting ends with a lot of self congratulatory remarks on the part of all.

Commentary

This episode clearly exemplifies much of the analogy of drama. The teacher understands that this little drama within the drama of schooling contains an important lesson for the drama of living. She plays the role of the director as she arranges the scene: the students sitting in a circle; the ground rules; the focus on the group problem.

Students are both actors and critics. They reflect on the drama, and then act it out again. By observing themselves in the conflict, they are able to see that it is not simply the ill will of the fifth graders that is to blame. The problem is partly a scheduling one. If they can solve that they will probably avoid fights. However, just to make sure, they will appoint some peers to take care of troublemakers.

Without going into an analysis at deeper levels, which would have been inappropriate to their level of development, the teacher encourages them to improvise a solution which calls upon their collaborative skills, rather than their combative skills. As with most contests of this kind, there are irrational elements to it: territoriality, male aggressiveness (probably culturally induced), power and control of a social situation to suit one's preference and convenience. Two opposite solutions usually present themselves in such a case: a violent contest of physical strength, or a resort to legal authorities to settle the dispute in favour of one side. In either case, there are winners and losers. The children, however, seek a solution that is fair to all sides, allowing everyone to be winners — or at least setting up a trial which has that as the goal.

We do not know what the outcome to this drama was. However it turns out, there will be lessons learned; the drama of living will have been 'schooled'. If the plan fails, many of the children will feel less inclined to attempt such cooperative efforts in the future. If it succeeds, they will be more likely to try them. More than likely, the attempt will have mixed results. A persistent teacher will continue to have them reflect on the outcomes, and rehearse the problem again for greater insight.

The episode, however, illustrates the building of character and the formation of a people. The youngsters are learning that being a community takes work and requires some sacrifices of selfish desires so that everyone has an opportunity to enjoy the common resources of the community. By coming up with the three person scheduling team and the patrol team, they are taking responsibility to deal with their own problems, rather than calling on the higher authorities to solve it for them. The episode also points out some possibilities for improvisation and rehearsal. The teacher might have gone further and had the youngsters rehearse a few probable scenes under the new arrangement, simply to anticipate new problems that might arise.

Discussion of the Findings

The six episodes represent a small sample of the huge variety of settings, circumstances, personalities, learning tasks, resources and creative approaches in the drama of schooling. The purpose of this small journey through various classrooms was to test the viability of the metaphors derived from the dramatic analogy. These episodes, at least, seem rather congenial to assessment based on the analogy. We find academic scripts, personal scripts, social scripts; we find some formation of character, some formation of a people; we find some improvisation, and in it a lively sense of significant learning taking place; we find some rehearsal for both the drama of schooling and the schooling of drama. Interestingly enough, we find no uniform formula: in every classroom we find unique illustrations of scripting, improvisation, coaching, directing and acting. So much seems to depend on the chemistry of people, topic, timing and setting.

The analogy instructs as well by its apparent absence, or by its partial expression. We see what appear to be opportunities lost, when the academic script might have been more easily related to the personal script of the students, when there might have been some time given over to schooling for living, not as an artificial intrusion on the integrity of the academic script, but as a natural consequence, or a perfect illustration of the academic script. We see teachers wrestling with the dilemma over coverage of prescripted material against the personal appropriation at a much greater depth of only some of the material. More often than not, teachers opt to cover the material, or to move on to the next part of their lesson plan, at the expense of reinforcing important learnings in the drama of living.

In this regard, the analogy raises important policy questions about the nature of the curriculum and about school-wide objectives. Teachers know from even a cursory attention to messages incessantly posted from the governor and the superintendent that they are expected to demand greater academic achievement from their students, achievement measurable by standardized tests. Small wonder, then, that they suppress their professional instinct to take time to attend to the lessons of living. Small wonder, then, as well, that issues concerning the quality of life disappear from the curriculum. And then we might ask what we have 'achieved' after all.

Chapter 11

Schooling as Drama: Concluding Reflections

One way of understanding the effort which this book represents is to situate it between the left and the right in the literature on school reform. The categories of left and right are themselves slippery categories. In general the critics on the left accuse the schools of being politically naive, or oppressive, or simply unconscious of reflecting the social contradictions inherent in the present political-economic order. The critics on the right accuse the schools of not attending to the passing on of the culture, of not developing respect for authority, of not nurturing habits of hard work, self restraint and traditional virtues associated in the past with 'character'.[1]

If the right were to use the language of drama, they would insist on the necessity of learning the conventions of the drama. With this general principle we would agree. We would go beyond the teaching of the conventions (language, cultural frameworks, values, traditions), however, to the need to use the conventions, and even to transform them, in the service of the demands of our present social and individual history. To teach social conventions as totally defining the social drama is a distortion of social history and a denial of the possibility and the right of a people to manage their own destiny.

As the left would have it, learning the conventions of the social drama is alienating. With this general principle we would agree. As Weber saw, however, engagement in any form of social life is alienating.[2] Engagement with others in any form of organized social life requires some surrender of autonomy, freedom, creativity. It is not, as Marx would have it, simply a matter of the workplace; social existence of itself brings alienation. The drama of social existence always involves the tension between the exercise of individual autonomy and freedom, and the demands of the conventions of social relations, as Becker has convincingly shown.[3]

Learning the conventions of the academic script, the bureaucratic script and the social script will lead to the experience of that tension. If the school labels that tension as unfounded, or worse, as something to be passively endured, it will only increase the sense of alienation. If, on the other hand, the school insists on the learning of the script as a necessary prerequisite to dealing with the alienations which it engenders, and expressly deals with those limitations and distortions of the script as the script is being learned, then it is beginning to school the drama of living.

The above positioning of the argument as falling in the middle of the implied extremes of the left and the right, however, is an easy sleight-of-hand. The scholars who conduct the arguments from the left and the right should be left to their important work. Without ignoring the debate, we shift the focus to action. There is a paralysis that sets in when reading the arguments of the right and the left. They are contesting the whole battlefield, using epoch-encompassing frames of analysis. We speak to educators working in particular, individual schools, with individual human beings. To be sure the argument strives to make a difference in the larger struggle for a better future of humankind. Working on the smaller stage, however, with the local players and their repertory of scripts, and joined with other colleagues who work on similarly small stages, perhaps collectively we can prepare enough young people who can rewrite the script from the bottom up.

The social drama is not something taking place somewhere entirely outside the walls of the school. The social drama and its personal reverberations are taking place in people. Educators are in the drama and the drama is in them. It is not as though they have a totally separate person who chooses now to play a role in an independent drama of schooling. In one sense they do not exist outside of this specific drama in which they find themselves. Moreover, who they are is defined within the drama both by the cultural script and by their choices of action within the script: accommodation, rebellion, deceit, creative exploration.

Educators create themselves by active involvement in the drama, or they find themselves externally shaped by the drama, usually in controlling and manipulative ways. They are passive in the drama at their own expense.

Other people in the drama will establish themselves as predominant actors at the cost of their self definition. Educators may choose to play in the drama by a form of autism, but their identity is still framed by that choice to be a disengaged critic of the drama. Choosing not to be involved is a form of dramatic action, with consequences at least as dramatic as involvement.

There are two ways to conduct the drama of schooling. One is to treat the production as the making of things (grades, test scores, achievement, victories, class ranks, skills, understandings, values). The other is to treat the production as making oneself and making a community. The second kind of making, of course is never completed; its very identity is at least as much in the making as in the product.[4] This form of the drama of schooling requires mutuality, discourse, exploration, trust. Those qualities only emerge in schools that agree to a shared enterprise of engaging the drama of living through the drama of schooling.

The drama is about human life, its density and depth, its multiform and continuous ambiguity, ambivalence and multivalence. We never experience it simply or wholly. Schools attempt to reduce this life to simpler terms: textbooks present definitions and formulas and divide things up in chapters. While this simplification of the world enables us to comprehend it in its uniform parts, we lose both the simultaneity of its complex dynamism and the shimmering moments of its fragile expression.[5] In studying the world as a static and disassembled thing, we lose both the world and ourselves, for in apprehending the world as pieces of information, we, too, are reduced to receptacles of pieces of information. In schools, we work on the world with a cruel scalpel, presuming we knew how to cut it apart and label it. All the while the world is working on us, not only nurturing our biological lives but shaping our very selves through the cultural bath of meanings in which we are immersed.

Thus disassembled, the world takes on an appearance of static stability. Yet the formulas and definitions and subdivisions are human constructs. Sometimes, if not always, those constructs have ideological significance, in presenting a view of how the world works. By the very labels used to express them, these constructs fix various people in static power relations within society. There are those 'employed' in the service economy. There are others who direct world trade. There are minorities; there are majorities, some of whom in specific cities are in the minority. There are criminals; there are law abiding citizens, some of whom are given five to ten year grace periods to 'be in compliance with the law'. Some people are on welfare; other people receive tax incentives, or tax write-offs. A 'healthy' economy requires five or six per cent unemployment — among the labor force, of course, not among corporate executives. Places, too, have different values: ghettos and suburbs, developed and undeveloped nations, zones of opportunity and private estates. Schools present the world as structured in certain ways, and imply that these structures are relatively permanent. They confidently define with deadly ignorance the limits of the drama.

Most schools would be hard pressed to throw out their curriculum, shaped by standard textbooks and district-wide guidelines. Nevertheless, it would be possible to begin in very ordinary classroom discussions to rehearse the alienation resulting from such prescripted views of the world, and thereby to open up space for improvised, experimental scripts that reconstruct the roles of the social drama. It does not require a third grade course in critical philosophy; it requires only that teachers encourage youngsters to reflect upon how the social drama currently works, and to explore the children's suggestions about rewriting the script. Such a rewriting of the script does not imply a wholesale rejection of the textbook script; rather, it implies playing the scenes in a variety of ways to minimize the damage and increase the humanity of the drama.

Children exposed to that kind of reflection and creative improvisation over the course of ten to twelve years would be more likely to continue their involvement in the renewal of the social drama, than would those who passively accept the unreflective roles assigned them by the script writers in the textbook industry. Teachers who integrate their roles in the drama of schooling with their roles in the drama of living will find their work far more meaningful than those who accept the schizophrenic separation of the two. Parents and school board members might have a clearer sense of a balanced continuum of priorities for the education of their children, if they understood the necessary connection between the schooling of the social drama and the drama of schooling.

Implications

The use of the analogy of drama in making sense of schooling is not the only way to look at schools. The argument in this book is that, if one adopts the perspective of a local, individual school, the analogy of drama is helpful. To be sure, the analogy may be more fully developed and refined by subsequent analyses. For the moment, however, we may be in a position to draw out some implications of the analogy for teacher preparation programs, for instructional analysis, for administrator preparation programs and for policy setting.

Teacher Preparation

Teacher preparation programs can be enriched by applying the analogy of drama to both the methods courses and the content courses. Although out of fashion, philosophy of education courses might be required or recommended as a way of getting prospective teachers to consider the basic purposes behind schools and behind their life's profession. Considering the schooling of the social drama as intrinsic to the drama of schooling might enliven the discussion of Plato's *Republic*, Rousseau's *Emile*, Dewey's *Democracy and Education*, Freire's *Pedogogy of the Oppressed*, or Alan Bloom's *The Closing of the American Mind*.

Beyond that, majors in Language Arts programs might be required to make more explicit relationships between their own lived experience, the literature they study, and the critical analysis of language as imbedded in ideology. Prospective science teachers ought to be familiar with the public policy implication of the science they study. Prospective social studies teachers ought to relate the historical and social sciences they are studying to an analysis of the conduct of the social drama of the present. They ought to study how the perspectives developed in their courses help them to understand their own feelings of alienation within the social drama. Prospective teachers in the arts ought to be reflecting on the relationship of the arts to the social drama, not necessarily as totally shaped by it, but at least as a response to it, perhaps in its deepest ambiguities.

Methods courses seem a natural place for the development of the coaching and directing skills required in the drama of schooling and the schooling of drama. Those skills, however, ought to be taught in a reflective practice framework. That is to say, those methods courses ought to explore how teaching is at a deep level an expression of autobiography. Being aware that one is teaching oneself enables teachers to recognize when they are imposing themselves on children; to recognize when that imposition is modelling and when it is demanding unauthentic imitation; to recognize when they have to restrain that impulse in order to encourage the youngsters to express their learning as their own autobiography; and to recognize when both teachers and learners have to silence their own limited understanding of the world in order to listen to the world afresh and let other living things and persons instruct them in their own unique language.

Specific coaching in the conduct of role playing, in the development of empathy and imagination, in script rewriting, improvisation, rehearsal and in restructuring and rehearsing a scene would also be called for in these methods courses. For those university professors unfamiliar with this kind of coaching, some creative improvisation with their students may be all that is required as long as it is conducted in the framework of reflective practice. Such improvisation would indeed model the lesson being taught.

Instructional Assessment

Instructional assessment, whether carried on by supervisors, administrators, or professional peers, could likewise use the frameworks derived from the analogy of drama. One of the lessons learned by extensive use of Hunter's model of teaching, or of the 'effective teaching' models is that they have provided supervisors, administrators and peer coaches with a common language to use with teachers when discussing classroom observations. Such common language enables both the observer and the observed to focus attention on certain teaching behaviors and to agree on how they were affecting the flow of the class.

It would be possible for teachers and observers of their instruction to explore the analogy of drama as it applies to that instruction. From the commentaries on the original classroom observation included in the previous chapter, it should be clear that the analogy does not impose a fixed formula of prescribed behaviors. Rather, using perspectives derived from the analogy (scripts, coaching, improvising, etc.), teachers and observers can perhaps arrive at some conclusions of their own about how they would like to improve some of the things they do in classrooms. The point is not to provide observers with new categories to judge and evaluate classroom instruction, but to provide teachers and observers with perspectives that facilitate the asking of fresh questions about what they want to do in their classrooms.

Administrator Preparation

Administrator preparation programs for building level administrators would explore the potential for leadership in administrators who work out of a sense of dramatic consciousness and who nurture that consciousness in the staff. Specifically, the implications of being a director of the drama ought to be explored, again within a reflective practice framework. Prospective principals and assistant principals need to explore in some depth the alienation felt by teachers and students due to excessive concentration on the bureaucratic script. They need to improvise ways to minimize the inescapable tension between the professional and bureaucratic scripts for the staff, and the ineradicable tension between the bureaucratic and personal scripts for everyone in the school, administrators included. Prospective administrators need to rehearse and then reflect upon how they can be authentic players in the drama, so that they do not lose their own humanity in the process of playing their roles.

Finally, those prospective administrators need to explore how they can articulate to the public that the drama at their school involves the schooling of the social drama. Given the plurality of views about how the social drama ought to be conducted, this will necessarily require of school administrators levels of diplomacy, courage and commitment to a continued involvement in this public discourse. The public, however, has to consider that schools are one of the few places in our society where the forms of the social drama can be explored and their consequences weighed; in a democratic society, this function of the school is essential for the ongoing renewal of the social drama itself. The schooling of the drama cannot be carried on without such public discussions, no matter how contentious they become. It is part of the drama of schooling. Administrator training programs rarely deal with this crucial leadership role in any programmatic way.

Policy

Policy making for schools in the current movement for reform has defined the social drama too narrowly, as exclusively an economic drama. Furthermore, even within this definition of the social drama, policy makers have not considered coaching youngsters in the skills of improvisation, a skill highly desirable in any industrial enterprise. The approach to the drama of schooling as the schooling of the social drama, however, restores a breadth to policy considerations, by which policy makers may consider restoring a degree of balance in the policy realm. Schooling as preparation for the world of work is a legitimate policy emphasis, to be sure. When it becomes the only policy emphasis, however, then it lends itself to such narrow applications as to defeat the very purposes it seeks to promote.

The social drama always has to deal with issues of alienation, whether that alienation has political, economic, cultural, or familial roots. Similarly the social drama involves the tension between individual autonomy, creativity and freedom, on the one hand, and the demands of membership in one or more social organizations. Schools must deal with these issues. Refusal to do so simply puts off dealing with them when their neglect has led to serious breakdowns in the social drama, breakdowns which are far more expensive to repair or even contain, later on. By considering the needs of the social drama and its ongoing renewal, policy makers for schools can encourage a curriculum and a pedagogy that attends to the multiform issues involved in the social drama. Attention to those multiform issues constitutes an investment in the future health of that social drama and indeed in the health of the drama of schooling itself.

Notes

1 For a good summary of these contrasting points of view, see Holtz, H., Marcus, I., Dougherty, J., Michaels, J. and Peduzzi, R. (Eds) (1989) *Education and the American Dream*, Granby, MA, Bergin and Garvey.

2 Eisenstadt, S. (1968) *Max Weber: On Charisma and Institution Building*, Chicago, University of Chicago Press, p. xv.

3 Becker, E. (1971) *The Birth and Death of Meaning*, 2nd ed., New York, The Free Press.

4 See Wexler, P. (1987) *Social Analysis of Education: After the New Sociology*, London, Routledge and Kegan Paul. pp. 174 ff.

5 For a development of this theme, see Starratt, R. (1989) 'Knowing at the level of sympathy: A curriculum challenge', *Journal of Curriculum and Supervision*, 4, 3.

Index